A MANUAL FOR
THE ART OF LIVING

A MANUAL FOR THE ART OF LIVING

*Some critical steps for building and assembling
a complete and purposeful life*

DR. HENDERSON BROME

A MANUAL FOR THE ART OF LIVING
SOME CRITICAL STEPS FOR BUILDING AND ASSEMBLING A COMPLETE AND PURPOSEFUL LIFE

iUniverse books may be ordered through booksellers or by contacting:

iUniverse
1663 Liberty Drive
Bloomington, IN 47403
www.iuniverse.com
844-349-9409

Because of the dynamic nature of the Internet, any web addresses or links contained in this book may have changed since publication and may no longer be valid. The views expressed in this work are solely those of the author and do not necessarily reflect the views of the publisher, and the publisher hereby disclaims any responsibility for them.

Any people depicted in stock imagery provided by Getty Images are models, and such images are being used for illustrative purposes only. Certain stock imagery © Getty Images.

ISBN: 978-1-6632-5571-6 (sc)
ISBN: 978-1-6632-5572-3 (e)

Library of Congress Control Number: 2023916307

Print information available on the last page.

iUniverse rev. date: 09/11/2023

CONTENTS

Acknowledgement vii

Foreward xi

Preface xiii

Chapter 1   Introduction 1

Chapter 2   Your Health is Your Greatest Asset 7

Chapter 3   Adversity and Failure Are Inevitable........ 13

Chapter 4   Avoid Destruction Highway.................... 21

Chapter 5   Contentment 26

Chapter 6   Choose Your Friends Wisely 33

Chapter 7   Choosing a Career 39

Chapter 8   Education and it's Importance 44

Chapter 9   Character is Your Road Map.................... 52

Chapter 10 Forgiveness 58

Chapter 11 Greed.. 66

Chapter 12 Gratitude 75

Chapter 13 Do Not Be Judgmental............................. 82

Chapter 14 Taking Stock of Your Life 91

Chapter 15 Time is your most precious gift, but it is
fleeting, use it wisely. 97

ACKNOWLEDGEMENT

I grew up in a household with my parents and twelve siblings. The experience of living in such a large family had its privileges but it was also fraught with many profound and stubborn challenges. The benefits of having several sisters and brothers automatically helped to temper and tame the egocentric and self-centered tendencies that are so prevalent among young people during this early period of development.

We learned very early how to share and care for each other. Moreover, we discovered quickly and out of necessity how to work collectively and collaboratively for our survival. The older siblings spontaneously accepted the responsibility to help the younger ones. Each of us had the opportunity to choose a mentor or role model from within our own clan rather than going outside of our home or from some other external source to seek help.

Older siblings were given permission by our parents to discipline the younger ones in order to keep us on the straight and narrow path. Already the older siblings were honing and developing skills that would prepare them for their own parenting in the future. In essence the positive experience in such an environment meant that our home was virtually a laboratory for training us how to become responsible and autonomous adults.

On the other hand, the challenge for providing for such a large family and household was extremely profound and ominous. The cost of caring for a household of fourteen persons was prohibitive. Our father was the sole person with an income. As a laborer within the plantation system his wages were totally inadequate to provide for such a large household. It is to the credit of our parents, a testament to their will, creativity and ingenuity that they developed a model of parenting and entrepreneurship that made the impossible possible. They demonstrated that they could defy and defeat the odds and above all overcome the insurmountable obstacles which threatened to trap them. They provided a model of parenting which stipulated that any semblance of successful parenting had to stem from a partnership. An unbreakable bond was necessary to address the daunting challenges of financial security.

Furthermore, in order to address the inadequate income, they developed a strategy to supplement that income by farming land which they owned. They cultivated sugar cane and vegetables and raised cows, sheep and pigs to sell in the marketplace. This required the full participation of the entire household with our mother being the "financial officer" It is important to note that during this time secondary education was not free. Parents had to pay for their children's education. We, the children had to participate in helping to pay for our education. Furthermore, our parents consistently instilled in us that education was the primary weapon to liberate us from the tentacles of poverty. It was an investment in our future. Again, this experience provided an ideal opportunity to teach several lessons about the importance of hard work, personal effort and responsibility. Our father's aim and goal were to ensure that his children grew to be self-sufficient, independent and autonomous adults. Unfortunately, he died before two of us finished high school - my brother and I were still in our early teenage years.

Many years before his death, he was constantly in hospital where he eventually died. His last words on his death bed addressed to our mother were "take care of Hendy and Val". These were powerful words that encapsulated and epitomized the depth of his mission and the purpose of our parents. They collectively took care of us, they loved us, they sacrificed their lives for us - such was the depth of their commitment and their perception of the nature and role of parenting. Not even the pangs and pain of imminent death could deflect him from his obligation to take care of his children.

Our father was buried twenty-four hours after his

death. The burial service was brief without any testimony of his noble deeds, no tribute or eulogy that expressed his contribution to his family. Our mother died twenty-six years later. We the members of the family were overwhelmed by the gravity of her loss and we could not muster the strength to express our love, appreciation and gratitude for her noble acts as a mother.

A public declaration of our parents' deeds and a proclamation of their insuperable acts as loving and caring parents have been the unfinished business of our family's agenda.

I am using the publication of this book as a medium to express on my behalf, as well as my sisters and brothers, our deepest love, appreciation and gratitude to our parents Leon and Constance Brome. As they rest from their labors and experience the peace of a job well done, we are confident that their life and legacy will live on in their grandchildren, great-grandchildren and for generations to come.

FOREWARD

To live authentic and fulfilling lives, we must be intentional. However, our fears and daily distractions often hinder us from making the best decisions for ourselves. In *A Manual for the Art of Living*, Dr. Henderson Brome provides practical advice on several areas of our lives that we tend to overlook, including our health, self-reflection, and gratitude. By sharing personal experiences and examples, Dr. Brome reminds us of simple steps we can take to improve upon our lives and the quality of our relationships. Each chapter provokes introspection and encourages readers to be proactive about creating better futures for themselves. Dr. Brome's message is timeless, especially for the youth, who tend to stumble - navigating life without having much guidance or wisdom. This book is a valuable roadmap for creating full and purposeful lives.

Lesley-Ann Giddings, Ph.D.
Assistant Professor of Chemistry, Smith College

PREFACE

Dr. Henderson Brome has observed that in many spheres of our lives we are provided with a manual of instruction to aid us in several activities. For instance, when we purchase an automobile, a home appliance or even furniture which requires assembling, each product is accompanied by a manual of instruction which supplies us with the precise and specific information relative to their operation and appropriate maintenance.

In many other areas, such as the workplace, manuals of instructions are usually made accessible to employees to provide them with information that will facilitate and enhance their job performance. The ultimate goal is to maximize the productivity and success of the entire enterprise.

Dr. Brome contends that while manuals of instruction are as ubiquitous as the air we breathe, the ultimate paradox is the fact that noticeably absent from our experience is the reality that there is no singular, consistent or cohesive guide which we can research to help us in assembling and constructing our lives so that we can reach optimum level of productivity. There is no compendium of information that will provide us with the necessary assistance as to how we should build our characters, construct our personalities and assemble each and every facet of our beings. What we ultimately wish to become is contingent upon how we live, and how we live is an art form. However, there is no manual for the art of living.

This book, "A Manual For The Art of Living" is an attempt to provide us with some critical steps for building and assembling a complete and purposeful life.

CHAPTER 1

INTRODUCTION

———⊷◈⊶———

The conceptualization of the title and content of this book came obstensively as a result of one of my regular and routine visits to the bank. The nature of the transaction of business on that occasion required me to consult with a customer service representative.

While the representative was processing and reviewing the information which I provided her, I casually glanced at a bookshelf in her office and immediately what caught my eyes, what aroused my attention and piqued my curiosity was a large spiral bound folder entitled, "A Manual for Customer Service Representatives". It is amazing that vacuous moments - such as waiting on someone - can invariably drive us to a place of inner reflection and provide us with an opportunity for deeper introspection. Two factors aroused my curiosity, the idea and concept of a manual and the intrinsic value and purpose of any manual.

While it is not normal for someone to ponder upon the idea of a manual and its usefulness, upon closer examination one quickly discovers that in almost every facet of our lives we use a manual without the consciousness of its importance. Its role is pivotal, it instructs, it enlightens, it guides and it facilitates. We could hardly survive without it. For instance, when we purchase an automobile, it comes with a manual for proper maintenance and operation. When we purchase such things as appliances there is the accompanying manual of instructions. In other instances, there is also a manual of instructions for assembling particular items.

The manual for maintenance and operation provides us with the necessary instructions about how to maintain and operate the object so that one can achieve optimum satisfaction. In the case of the manual for assembling, one is provided with meticulous and sequential step by step instructions in order to make the object operable or functional. Some of us may discover from bitter experience that if we fail to follow the precise instruction that at best it could be a frustrating experience or at worst it could damage the object thus making it inoperable.

One can safely assume what the content of a manual of instruction for customer service representatives would entail. No doubt such a manual is designed to facilitate the work of the customer service representatives and to educate them about all aspects of their roles. It is designed to enhance and maximize their performance. More specifically there is no doubt that the role of the customer service representative is a dual one. His or her task is to facilitate the customers dealings with the bank and to provide the kind of environment and positive experience that will satisfy the customer. Secondly the customer service representative is also an advocate and an ambassador for the business which he or she represents. Providing a hospitable environment may be the best marketing tool for the success of such business.

In the final analysis a knowledgeable customer service representative is critical for the vitality and success of the business he represents. In the case of the bank, his depth of knowledge could inevitably maximize its potential, making it more competitive and ensuring its growth and productivity.

The result of this inner introspection on such a simple idea of a manual and its purpose led me to a profound epiphany in my thinking. It suddenly dawned on me that in every area of our lives there will be occasions for the use of a manual of instruction for almost any product – from the purchase of an automobile to something as simple as the assembling of a toy for a child.

Yet one of the real paradoxes of life is the fact that for the most important aspect of our life, there is no manual, no compendium of information that one can refer to for guidance about how to live, how to construct our lives, how to assemble our personalities and above all how to build and structure our characters. There is no manual that provides us with the requisite information that aids us in becoming fully functional individuals. What we ultimately want to become is contingent upon how we live and how we live is an art form. Yet there is no one place of reference that will provide us with the instructions as to the operation of our lives. There is no manual of instructions for the art of living. Tragically, we have left it to luck and chance, trial and error to help us assemble our lives, operate our lives as we navigate the complex route of life's pilgrimage. In the past, we have relied on several institutions for instructions and guidance for the development and direction of our lives but there is no coordination, consistency or certainty in the availability of that knowledge. Traditionally, the family was the premiere and most invaluable resource that we could depend on to inculcate the values that would aid in the assembly of our lives but the family and the family structure have dramatically changed. The contemporary family is in a state of crisis as the high level of divorce has taken its toll on the stability of the family. In response to the fragility of family life, many have espoused the theory that it takes a village to raise a child as a remedy to the rapid and radical changes of the family. However, from a demographical standpoint there is no such thing as a village, as people have become more mobile, transient and nomadic. Anonymity and rugged individualism have undermined any meaningful sense of community.

The school used to be an extension of the family, sharing a partnership and reflecting a common ethos and common values. They were like symbiotic twins serving to impart the basic values of the community. However, values are rapidly shifting, and simultaneously casting doubt that there are universal and uniform values. Furthermore, many of our schools are under siege by violence and crime.

Religious institutions used to play an indispensable role in the formation of individuals. They were an integral part of the process of providing vital resources to help us face the challenges of life. However, many religious institutions are failing to capture the attention or the allegiance of many particularly the youth. Religious institutions are failing to capture the interests of many people as they wrestle with what they perceive as an artifact of the past, that is both archaic, obsolete and above all irrelevant. With the rapid diminution of the influence of these institutions, what other source can we rely on to fill the void left by them? Where can we find the appropriate information that can help us assemble our lives so that we can live them more creatively and productively? What are some of the basic and fundamental imperatives which we need to be cognizant of and which we can apply in our lives in order to prevent us from becoming dysfunctional persons?

This book "A Manual for the Art of Living" is but a modest attempt to coordinate and to collate the nuggets of advice which were passed on to us through our pastors and parents, our grandparents and teachers who were all agents of the institutions of family, faith and school. I believe strongly that if we follow some basic and fundamental precepts and principles of life contained in this manual, that we may become more productive persons with lives that are whole, complete and above all fulfilling.

CHAPTER 2

YOUR HEALTH IS YOUR GREATEST ASSET

I t is not surprising that if you were to take a survey and ask some people what are their goals in life that their health would either take a very low priority or be totally omitted from their personal agenda. It is not that they don't want to be healthy or that they don't care about their health but rather, like so many people they take it for granted. Unfortunately taking one's health for granted leads to indifference, ignorance, neglect and can be costly in terms of suffering and even death. What are your goals or ambition in life? The answer is usually predictable. It entails a good education, a career, a profession or a job that can provide financial security, the acquisition of a house and the beginning of a family. Such a response does force one to ask a very critical question. To what end is a good education, a reliable job that can provide financial security, the acquisition of a home and a family, if one is constantly sick or too sick to enjoy any of them?

Far too many of us suffer from the syndrome of misplaced priorities. I have a tendency when enquiring about someone's health to do so in the form of a quiz. I do so particularly with those who own a car. When last did you take your vehicle for a service? Almost all of them can provide me with an immediate answer with meticulous precision. They know which service is for the next appointment and what are the particular parts of the car that must be serviced based upon the mileage or duration of time. They adhere tenaciously and meticulously to the instructions provided in the owner's manual for maintenance and operation. They know intuitively that failure to follow the proper procedures can result in costly repairs and permanently damage the vehicle. Neglect can be costly. But there is a follow up question that I usually ask. When last did you have an annual physical examination? Invariably I then begin to discover that many of my eloquent and articulate friends have a severe case of stuttering, or I have to listen to some bizarre rationalization of their apathy and indifference to their personal health. It is amazing that they never see the correlation between the maintenance of a vehicle an object that is made of steel and iron and the human body that is made of flesh and blood. It seems as though they are oblivious to the appropriate awareness that their bodies need the same kind of consistent and precise care and maintenance in order to function at an optimal level. This requires that we must not wait to become a passive patient in a doctor's office or in an emergency room but rather that we have made a proactive decision to become an aggressive advocate and participant in the maintenance of our bodies and the wellness of our beings. It is to be noted that when I speak of health and wellness that I am referring to the totality of human health and wellness, all facets of our being — physical, mental and emotional.

Like most things in life which require maintenance to be effective, our bodies need an annual examination. Having our bodies "serviced" must become an annual ritual, a regimen and a routine. An annual physical examination does not simply mean undergoing routine or specific tests but consultation with your primary care physician who may be able to foresee certain factors which might make one susceptible to some illness and accordingly advise you to make certain changes and adjustments to some areas of your life. The key however of becoming an aggressive advocate in one's healthcare and its management is knowledge. One does not have to be a doctor, or one does not have to 'play doctor' or become a professional hypochondriac but it is imperative for everyone to have some basic and rudimentary knowledge about our bodies and how they function. In this respect nutrition is a vital component in the management and care of our health. We need food not only to prevent hunger. If that were the case, then one could eat anything and everything. We need food because it is the primary source of the nutrients which our bodies require. Our bodies need basic nutrients which we get from different foods and we must be conscious of the foods we eat, the nutrients they provide and the portions that are necessary to meet the basic requirements. Implicit in the old adage that you are what you eat is the notion that you should know what you eat. One should search for and learn about the importance of nutrition and the impact of one's eating habits.

The next building block in the maintenance and management of one's health is adopting a healthy lifestyle. There are many facets to this building block. One cannot overstate nor overemphasize the importance of exercise. It helps in all areas of our lives. It is important for exercise to be regular and consistent for it to be effective. One must refrain from the use and abuse of illicit drugs because they can take a heavy toll on one's health. Stress can also have a negative impact on almost all aspects of our being, physical and mental. Consequently, we must learn to avoid stressful situations and persons who are progenitors of conflict and who are prone to produce toxic situations.

At some point in our lives, we may be required to take prescription drugs in order to control or manage some conditions such as hypertension, diabctes, high cholesterol and others. Again our approach to taking prescription drugs should be predicated on knowledge. We should consult our doctor or pharmacist about all aspects of the prescribed drugs. We should read the labels and become knowledgeable and conversant about their benefits as well as side effects. Some people have the naive perception that if they are prescribed a drug, that they should begin to experience some immediate improvement in their condition. However a drug may have some side effects such as dizziness which may occur in the initial stage until the body makes some adjustment. Without this awareness some people discontinue taking the drug because "it is not working", or "it is making me feel sick". Such actions can have dangerous, and sometimes deadly consequences. It is very important to use drugs as they are prescribed. In this context knowledge and communication are the operative words.

Closely aligned with this is the fact that people should know some basic and rudimentary ideas especially numbers that relate to their health. Know their significance and what they represent. In essence, I am pleading for everyone to become engaged in the management of their health. You cannot afford to be a spectator in this area. Unfortunately, some people know more about their numbers from the credit bureau, than their numbers pertaining to their health - blood pressure, cholesterol and triglycerides. The recognition of symptoms and the timely reporting of them can save your life.

Finally, there are certain genetic and heredity factors which put some people at greater risk for certain illnesses. In some racial or ethnic groups the incidence of certain ailments are higher. Research has shown that if there is a history of cancer in one's family, then the rate of susceptibility is significantly higher and more consistent than in other populations We should learn more about those factors that could potentially place us at higher risk and take the necessary steps to engage in preventive therapy.

The foregoing information is not meant to provide an exhaustive account of all things related to one's personal health management. It is not meant to provide medical advice as such advice should come from a physician. This information is intended to provide practical hints that should stimulate one to become engaged in the advocacy and management of one's own health care.

CHAPTER 3

ADVERSITY AND FAILURE ARE INEVITABLE

———⊷◦⊶———

"The man who makes no mistakes is the man who never does anything". Theodore Roosevelt

There is almost an innate fear in the heart of each one of us about the prospect of having to deal with failure and disappointment at some stage of our lives. This fear begins as early as infancy. It becomes very evident as a toddler begins to crawl and walk or to babble and talk. Children can become very frustrated when they fall or when they experience some difficulty to verbalize something or to express some feeling. However, the intervention of an adult can provide the guidance which gives them the resource to try again and again. The damage of this fear and its consequence can affect and follow individuals throughout their lives. Through the socialization process we have been conditioned to believe that failure, setbacks, mistakes and disappointments are symptoms of some form of weakness and inadequacy is us. In all instances these are viewed and perceived as negative experiences. When this occurs in us such feelings can inevitably lead to a reduction of trust and a loss of confidence in ourselves. This invariably undermines the self-esteem which is a vital attribute of our character that enables us to function as autonomous human beings.

Traditionally we have been led to believe that there are certain safeguards and initiatives which we can employ that will immunize us from life's challenges and can insulate us from the devastating effect of failure, misfortune and adversity. We have come to believe that a good education, a productive career and profession, access to power and material possessions are critical factors which can either exempt us or enable us to overcome the painful experiences of life. Yet history and experience have demonstrated that neither knowledge and a career, fame and fortune, power and possessions while undoubtedly being very helpful in providing some level of comfort and resources will exempt us from the pain and anguish of life's disappointments, setbacks, trials and tragedies. Many who have invested in these conventional "safeguards" will find themselves ill-equipped and unprepared to cope with both the countless assaults on their dreams and aspirations as well as the negative vicissitudes of their life's experiences. I cannot think of any scenario in life that would enable us to avoid such inescapable realities such as sickness, loss in its many forms and manifestations, broken relationships, loneliness and isolation, aging, disloyalty and disappointment. In all of these instances, position, possession and profession will undoubtedly fall short of providing us with any remedy for these challenges. In our thirst and quest for healing, wholeness, friendship and companionship we will quickly discover that these cannot be purchased nor can they be attained by material resources.

In a world that has become more and more conscious of the impact of nutrition on our health, we have become more and more familiar with such terms as caffeine free, sugar free, sodium free, fat free, in which harmful properties can be extracted from some foods but this cannot be replicated in our personal lives. Life will never be trouble or problem free. Adversity touches everyone. Trouble lurks all around us and we cannot extract it from our environment. It's a universal experience that stalks and assaults us. In a biblical story, on the occasion of his farewell discourse to his friends and followers, Jesus poignantly forewarned them, that they would not escape trouble; in fact, they should expect it, "In this world you will have trouble but do not fear". Jesus would have been a false prophet if he had tried to sell them a pipe dream of a life without challenges.

In November 1992, the Queen of England, Queen Elizabeth II, considered to be one of the richest persons in the world, with an equal amount of fame and popularity revealed to the whole world that it was a most horrible year – "annus horribilis". Marking the 40th anniversary of her accession as Queen, she remarked "…1992 is not a year on which I shall look back on with undiluted pleasure…it has turned out to be an annus horribilis. I suspect that I am not alone in thinking it so…". The experience of that horrible year came in rapid succession. In March, her second son Andrew announced the separation from his wife which consequently ended in divorce, in April, her daughter Princess Anne got divorced from her husband, in May the publication of a book exposed the turmoil between her eldest son Prince Charles and his wife Princess Diana which eventually ended in divorce. Those family crises were followed by a devasting fire at Windsor castle, one of her favorite properties. The horrifying experience of the Queen of England is a compelling reminder that none of us, not even the richest and most powerful among us, will be able to avoid the damaging consequences of misfortune. Adversity is a universal experience of the human condition. Each one of us will experience in some form or another, a horrible year, a challenging month, an uncertain time, a disappointing moment but we need not capitulate to cynicism or surrender to fatalism. Adversity brings within its wake and offers us opportunities to be grasped and lessons to be learnt. An ancient Romanian proverb asserts that adversity makes a man wise not rich. Nowhere is this portrayed in a very compelling way than in the expression of the Senior Duke in William Shakespeare's "As You Like It". The rivalry between two wealthy brothers, the Senior Duke and his younger brother, Frederick, ended in the banishment of the senior to the forest of Arden. It was a most difficult time for the senior duke who was exiled from the luxury and comfort of a wealthy existence deposed from his status as heir, deprived of his wealth and stripped of his dignity. His situation is also compounded even by his exposure to the fierce conditions of the weather. He bemoans, "the Winter's wind that bites upon his body until he shrinks with cold". Yet in those extreme and trying situations he declared emphatically and unapologetically that he would not change them. Even in these dire circumstances he has discovered an intrinsic goodness in them. He declared that he can put these adverse situations to productive use. He contends that in every ugly situation in life we can find a jewel of hope and restoration. Above all that we can find lessons and messages from the landscape of our emotional life. "Sweet are the uses of adversity which like a toad, ugly and venomous, wears yet a precious jewel in its head. And this my life, exempt from public haunt, found tongues in trees, books in the running brooks, sermons in stones and good in everything. I would not change it." [*Act II, Scene I*]

The duke in essence describes in great detail that

adversity has been a great teacher in showing him the many profits and benefits of the experience of misfortune. Adversity brought him to a point where he discovered goodness in the most trying and painful times of his life and above all he would not change them for anything.

Adversity can force us to search for the jewel, the precious jewel, the positive element in all the ugly and threatening circumstances of our lives. The paradox of life is that in all the bitter experiences which we face we can discover the sweetness of hope. To put it in colloquial terms, when life offers us a lemon we need not scorn its bitterness we can turn it into lemonade. Adversity is both transformative and redemptive.

The Duke discovered that the lessons to be learnt from adversity are exhaustive and ubiquitous. That even under the most brutal and inhospitable conditions of the forest which could have been life threatening he found a message in this most hostile environment. He found tongues in trees - the trees communicated to him a message of hope. He found books in the running brooks which offered him the wisdom not to succumb to despair but to develop the patience to embrace the alternative that our pain is never lasting but transitory. As the psalmist asserts, "Heaviness may endure for a night, but joy comes in the morning." We must embrace the philosophy that for every night of darkness there is a sunrise that is pregnant with hope and expectation.

Finally the exiled and deposed duke found sermons in stones. A sermon can be used to challenge and comfort, exhort and enlighten. A stone can have a dual purpose. It can be used to hurt, harm, maim or even kill someone but a stone can also be used constructively to build and rebuild. When adversity enters our space and many stones are thrown or hurled at us, the immediate response is the temptation to choose bitterness, revenge, anger and self-pity all of which have the potential to lead us on a path of self destruction. On the other hand we can use the stones of adversity as building blocks and stepping-stones to rebuild and reconfigure our lives. To use another colloquial term every setback which we face in life is but a setup for a comeback. Every setback is but an occasion and an opportunity for restoration and renewal.

Adversity can be an apprenticeship in character building whereby we can hone the skills to overcome the dangers, difficulties and disappointments of life. The noted Greek philosopher Heraclitus remarked that character is destiny. He emphasized that character or even fate is not determined and shaped by external forces, rather a person's character is determined and shaped by the inner attributes of one's character. Paul in his letter to the Romans tells us that the attributes of character such as endurance, perseverance and hope will not fail us during times of trial, pain, suffering and adversity. "We also boast in our sufferings knowing that suffering produces endurance and endurance produces hope and hope does not disappoint us" I can bear personal witness to the fact that like others I have experienced some measure of disappointments and adversity in my life. While I would not wish to relive them, I have found that I have learnt from them and have been strengthened by them. Patience, perseverance and persistence all germinate from the seeds of adversity.

To anyone who is currently experiencing adversity and pain, before you become overwhelmed by guilt and consumed with anger and bitterness, search for the lessons and the message hidden within them and you will discover the patience, hope and strength to transcend and conquer the pain of the moment and experience the promise of tomorrow.

Remember there can be good in everything.

CHAPTER 4

AVOID DESTRUCTION HIGHWAY

There is a way that seems right to a man but the end thereof is death. Proverbs Chapter 14, Verse 12

I grew up in a family with twelve siblings by any socio-economic barometer we would have met the classification of being poor, disadvantaged and underprivileged. We were truly a family of poverty and acquainted with want. But what made a profound difference was the fact that we were privileged to have parents who did not subscribe to the fallacious thinking that poverty was synonymous with powerlessness. They believed firmly, and instilled in us daily, that poverty, far from being a handicap would be the motivator that could emancipate us from the conditions of deprivation and insignificance. Our parents were our most powerful advocates who constantly inculcated in us that while we were marginalized by lack of material possessions that our potential was not minimized nor circumscribed. We were not heirs to any inheritance, we were the beneficiaries of a birthright that no one could take from us – we could be masters of our minds, custodians of our characters and architects of our ambitions and future. They told us that the preeminent means that could secure our exodus from poverty was through the development of our character and above all that a sound education would be a passport to success and a life of purpose and productivity. In this context they were prepared to make any sacrifice, to deny themselves to ensure that their children accomplished their dreams and goals. Secondary education was not free and it is obvious that their attempt to pay for the education of their children served only to underscore the depth of their sacrifice. Their sacrifice was so transparent and compelling that it had a dual impact on us.

Firstly, their sacrifice spoke volumes about their commitment to the advancement of their children and was indeed a most eloquent expression of their love. This was truly affirming and cannot be discounted. Secondly, it fostered in us the determination not to disappoint them nor to deviate from the goals which they helped us to forge. It further nourished in us the feeling that we should succeed not only for our own gratification and personal accomplishment but that our success would lay the foundation for a day when we would be able to repay them by making a contribution to improving their lives as well. One unintended by-product of this was that it helped us to manage and transcend the egocentric behavior that is so prevalent among aspiring youth.

Our parents taught us about the importance of setting goals for our lives. They encouraged us to dream and to construct a blueprint for our lives and our future. They instilled in us that nothing can be accomplished without effort and hard work. It is as if they were mirroring the charge and challenge of the abolitionist Frederick Douglass when he remarked "people may not get all they work for in this life, but they must certainly work for all they get". With all of these precepts and principles which they preached and practiced in their words and by their examples they were pointing us to a way by which we could accomplish our goals – they were delineating a road map to success.

Our mother who stayed at home caring for such a large family was quite naturally the one who maintained discipline. In this respect, communication was her greatest asset. She counselled, challenged and comforted us. Her harshest tone came when she uttered the words, "you are on your way to destruction highway" or "you better not go down destruction highway". She reserved her harshest reprimand when she observed that we were engaged in behavior that was antithetical to the covenant of self-empowerment which we vowed to uphold. According to her any action which sought to endanger, jeopardize or derail us from realizing our dreams and aspirations was a clear indication that we were on destruction highway.

In essence it was a road to self-destruction and a prescription for our demise. The road to self-empowerment demands hard work, discipline, struggle, perseverance and personal responsibility that reminds us that effort- our own effort and not entitlement will be the formula for personal success. On the other hand, the road to self-destruction also known as destruction highway is both seductive and deceptive. It dupes and deceives us into thinking that there are short cuts to achieving our goals and the road signs provide only directions that lead to death and destruction. An old biblical proverb warns us about the destructive nature of such a highway." There is a way that seemeth right unto a man but the end thereof is the way of death"

All of us have dreams, ambitions and aspirations in some form or another about achieving our destiny. However, it is vitally important for all to have a well-defined road map which charts the course for reaching this destination. There are critical choices which no one can make for us and which we must make for ourselves. We must reject the enticement to opt for easy street which demands no effort nor skills, which denigrates personal initiative, and which eventually leads to apathy and aimlessness. These are the precursors of defeat. We must reject the lure of the alternate route which offers a shortcut because we will quickly learn that on life's highway there is no express lane to success. Shortcuts only lead to detours and cul-de-sacs that will short-change your opportunities and options and short circuit your dreams.

Finally, the realization of our dreams and the accomplishment of our goals what we ultimately become – will be contingent not upon what we have inherited or what has been bestowed upon us but by the choices we make, the efforts which we expend and above all the road which we choose.

CHAPTER 5

CONTENTMENT

⟶◆⟵

One attribute of a person's character which is vitally important for the wellbeing of an individual is the attribute of contentment. The general concept of contentment is usually defined as the emotional state of satisfaction and fulfilment. Many people have viewed it as a preeminent quality that gives an individual a sense of accomplishment. When Socrates was asked, who is the wealthiest man, he responded "…he who is content with least, for contentment is nature's wealth." In William Shakespeare's King Henry VI, content is described as the crown of his heart. "My crown is in my heart, not in my head, not decked with diamonds, nor to be seen: my crown is called content, a crown it is that seldom kings enjoy". Benjamin Franklin, one of the founding fathers of the United States of America has been credited with the following statement "contentment makes poor men rich, discontent makes rich men poor".

The Apostle Paul became a mentor to Timothy, a young man who became a Bishop at a very early age. Paul provided Timothy with very sound and comprehensive advice both personally and professionally. Figuring prominently in this advice was his insistence that Timothy should acquire, nourish, develop and maintain a feeling of contentment which would undoubtedly redound to his success. "Godliness with contentment is great gain. For we brought nothing into the world, and we can take nothing out of it." Here Paul urges and indeed warns this young man at this critical stage of his career as he pursues his goals and dreams that he should do well to remember that among the gains which he will make that the greatest of them will be contentment if he pursues it. Paul was very emphatic to remind Timothy that as he pursues his dream the temptation for power and possession is more potent and prevalent but they both have an expiration date "for we brought nothing into this world and it is certain that we can take nothing out of it". Later, on another occasion, Paul would use his own personal example and experience to encourage a community in distress struggling with adversity and uncertainty to overcome their challenges by following his example. He proclaimed that he had faced similar crises in his life, but he was able to conquer them through the balance which contentment generates. He pointed to the value and secret of contentment. "For I have learned to be content in whatever situation I am in. I know both how to live in the humblest circumstances, and how to have far more than enough. In everything and in all things, I have learned the secret of being well fed and of being hungry, of having more than enough and of having less than enough."

In all of these instances from Socrates, Shakespeare, the Apostle Paul, Benjamin Franklin and others contentment is viewed and valued as an emotional state that all should strive to attain. It is perceived as man's greatest gain, nature's wealth, the crown of one's existence. It is the state of mind, the emotional equilibrium that gives us, imbues us with serenity and peace of mind not only in times of prosperity but also in times of adversity and tribulation. Conversely, however, while there are many who extol the virtues and benefits of contentment there are many others who view it in a negative light. They do not see contentment as the arsenal of man's weaponry to deal with the struggles of life and to achieve a measure of happiness. One prominent critic of the virtue of contentment, C. Frederick Crum, has opined that contentment is the enemy of greatness. According to him it is antithetical to success, it stymies ambitions and stunts growth. He contends that contentment is a foe of happiness, and that happiness is achieved through a continuous competition and urge to succeed. Contentment is a liability to human progress. The following remarks manifest the depth of his opposition. "In my world you are either in a state of improvement or in a state of decline. There is no plateau.

There is no contentment. Happiness is determined by growth and movement, success and movement in a positive direction not contentment with the status quo. By nature we are all born to compete, if we did not have that inborn trait, our species could have become extinct a long time ago."

Even a superficial analysis of this thinking reveals the fallacy of his distortion of the true meaning and nature of contentment. He views contentment as being synonymous with complacency and containment. Like many others who share this misconception of contentment he vigorously contends that it is the enemy of ambition It is virtually an attempt to abridge one's aspirations, derail and diminish one's dreams and of course to constrict and circumscribe the contours of one's vision. In essence the supporters of this negative view of contentment not only imply but categorically contend that it means settling for less than one is capable of achieving, in short minimizing one's potential Such a distorted view of the meaning of contentment has forced them to reach several erroneous conclusions. Firstly, that life is a perpetual competition and contest and happiness is derived from being competitive at all times. If we follow this trend of thinking, then it is fair to ask when is there a place or an occasion to pause and to appreciate and celebrate any victory and success? The incessant and endless urge to compete cheats us of the opportunities to celebrate and cherish the victories and triumphs of our lives.

Secondly, we may also ask, what happens to us when we fail to win, when we fail to succeed or simply when we are unable to compete? This thinking would force anyone to view themselves as a liability and as a useless person. Should we internalize this the emotional toll could be costly. We would easily be overwhelmed by guilt, self-doubt, a feeling of unworthiness and a lack of self-esteem. There is no doubt that ambition has been described as one of the most motivating forces in a person's life. It has been credited for being the critical factor in ensuring a person's success. However, unbridled and unchecked ambition can easily degenerate and metastasize into inordinate greed and avarice which will inevitably destroy and undermine any feeling of success. In fact, in William Shakespeare's Macbeth ambition has been described as the disease of the soul. In the pursuit of power and position, an individual stands in danger of allowing his ambition to devolve into irrationality.

It is a truism that ambition is a prerequisite for success. The success which one attains from ambition generally leads us to the proverbial fork in the road with two paths contentment or greed from which we must make a choice. If we choose greed, we become obsessed with hoarding and grabbing for more things, more power, wealth and status The lust and thirst for more will never be satisfied because irrational greed possesses us and dominates our thinking. If ambition is a disease of the soul then greed is a pollution of the heart. The success of a polluted heart does not allow us to share or to care. A polluted heart has no room for compassion. Persons with a polluted heart have no room for compassion. They are totally engaged in stockpiling their loot and enlarging their warehouse in order to accommodate more stuff.

Contentment, on the other hand, brings a healthy balance to the human experience. It upholds ambition and success as very important for anyone to function efficiently and effectively. On the other hand, it rejects the idolizing of things and provides us with the space and time to count our blessings, appreciate our gains and to celebrate our victories. Contentment balances this by forewarning us and making us aware of the fact that these by-products of success such as power, wealth and possessions are not permanent. In an environment that glorifies power and possessions we are reminded that we can lose them and yet be contented in the process. This was the observation made by Professor Dr. Henri Nouwen in his book "Finding My Way Home". He said, "...we live in a culture that measures the value of the human person by degrees of success and productivity. What is your title? How much money do you make? How many friends do you have? What are your accomplishments? How busy are you? What do your children do? But it is important for us to remember that as we grow older our ability to succeed in this way gradually diminishes. We lose our titles, our friends, our accomplishments and our ability to do many things, because we begin to feel weaker, more vulnerable and more dependent. Do we dare to look at weakness as an opportunity to become fruitful?" Professor Nouwen affirms that even in such situations we can still live with purpose because our usefulness is not measured by our ability to compete.

CHAPTER 6

CHOOSE YOUR
FRIENDS WISELY

———————⟫◆⟪———————

Building and shaping one's life require many variables. Very prominent among those variables is the need for genuine friendship which is usually described as a distinctively personal relationship that is grounded in concern on the part of each friend for the welfare of the other. In essence, friendship is a mutual relationship between people that is far deeper than mere casual acquaintances. It is widely held that friendship is one of the strongest forms of interpersonal bond which supersedes most human associations. Moreover, it is widely accepted that its benefits touch persons at all stages of their lives from childhood, adolescence and adulthood. The experiences of companionship as well as the emotional support which it provides can contribute immeasurably to the mental and physical health of individuals.

It is my personal and humble conviction that irrespective of one's station or standing in life that having a friend and being a friend can contribute immensely to one's fulfilment and wholeness. The ability to build and forge friendships is being challenged by many facets and factors of modernization. Modernization has facilitated the movement of people. People not only travel with ease, but they are no longer wedded to any particular community. They are more migratory and nomadic in their existence and the resultant casualty is the sense of belonging and community.

The acknowledgement of the need for friendship couldn't be more urgent at a time in which loneliness and isolation have become an epidemic on a global scale. Research conducted in the United Kingdom reveals that over nine million people in the United Kingdom say that they are always or often lonely. The research further stressed that loneliness and social isolation are harmful to our health. The results of this research have prompted the British government to establish a Ministry of Loneliness in order to confront this challenge of loneliness which plagues its people. This sense of isolation and loneliness is not limited to the elderly. Indeed, it is prevalent and pervasive in every age group particularly among the youth who is profoundly influenced by the digital phenomenon. An article in the New York Post, citing a recent survey by a market research company, claimed that one in five millennials are lonely and have no friends. It further claimed that social media savvy millennials make up the loneliest generation in America.

A research study conducted by the University of Manchester in the United Kingdom has revealed that young people feel loneliness more intensely than any other age group. For instance, 40% of people aged 16-24 say that they feel lonely compared with 29% of persons aged 65-74. The research also found that those who reported feeling the loneliest tended to have more "online" only friends on platforms such as Facebook. Within this environment and culture friendship has become such an abstract and remote concept that many young people concede that they not only have no friends but more tragically they do not know how to become friends.

Social media which is a by-product of technological advancement has made life more impersonal. When it is paired with the effects of modernization that has accelerated the pace and movement of people, many have been left isolated, alienated and estranged from each other. In such a context, people have virtually lost their sense of neighborliness. This situation is further compounded by the fact that the pool from which we choose our friendships is rapidly shrinking - due in part to the rigid lines of demarcation which separate people - not only in the traditional sense of gender, race or religion but in such areas as ideology, income and social status.

It should now become clear that it is imperative that we must re-learn not only how to choose friends but to have an unambiguous perception of the intrinsic nature and qualities of friendship. We must resist the notion of applying friendship to casual acquaintances and superficial associations for that is to undermine and diminish the true depth and meaning of friendship. For instance, networking which requires us to interface with others in our dealings with them should not be construed as a form of friendship. One's engagement in business or in one's workplace does not automatically mean that such configuration in our relationship can be equated with real friendship. Genuine friendship is significantly deeper and more consequential. In fact, one ancient proverb informs us that the bond of some friendships can be stronger than that of a sibling. "A person who has friends must show himself friendly; but there is a friend that sticks closer than a brother." Genuine friendship is based upon honor and trust. This means that the relationship is durable and dependable. A friend loves at all times, not only in prosperity but also in adversity. The real test of true and authentic friendship is when it requires us to make sacrifices or when it makes demands on us that are inconvenient. This honor and trust in friendship extend also to when the friendship has been breached and requires understanding and forgiveness. Authentic friendship requires the ability to forgive. The test of true friendship is the ability and willingness to forgive.

Both from words as well as actions, the benefits of friendships are very profound. However, it is important to note that the poor choice of friends can have a detrimental and damaging effect on our personalities. There is a biblical admonition that warns us about the devasting effects of the wrong friends. Such friends can also have a bad influence on our moods and our emotions. Persons who are purveyors of negativity and peddlers of pessimism can be contagious and any interaction with them will immediately infect us. The safest and most potent form of immunization is to avoid any meaningful or lasting relationship with them. That is why many parents warned their children to refrain from bad company and to make wise choices as it relates to their friends. It is critical that we screen those whom we desire to be our friends. Equally important is the fact that we should also examine ourselves about our ability to be a friend to others. Friendship must be mutual.

The effects of friends on our lives can be so profound that the choices of friends cannot be left to chance or random selection. The purposeful attempt to incorporate someone into our lives with such a degree of intimacy must be done, with deliberate introspection. Choosing a friend should be one of the most consequential choices of our lives. We do not get the chance to choose our parents, our siblings, our co-workers and colleagues, nor even our neighbors. The opportunity to choose our friends must be executed with wisdom. We must choose our friends wisely. Friendship can generate growth in both individuals who share that experience. While we may choose a person with similar interests and values, sameness and similarity alone can generate stagnation and stunt growth.

The false experience of trying to make a friend a clone of yourself can lead to deep frustration. The role of a friend must not be restricted to that of being a cheerleader. A genuine friend should be able to applaud as well as admonish us. This should not offend us because genuine friendship comes from a place that is always affirming. "Faithful are the wounds of a friend, his sharpest reproof proceed from an upright and truly loving and faithful soul. He is known by his good and faithful counsel as well as his reasonable rebukes."

CHAPTER 7

CHOOSING A CAREER

———◆———

"The meaning of life is to find your gift and the
purpose of life is to give it away" Pablo Picasso

O ne of the most important decisions which a person
can make for the direction of one's life is the
choice of a career, occupation, profession or vocation.
It is imperative that each of us should try to make every
effort and expend the maximum energy to discover our
unique talents, acknowledge them as a gift and develop
them not only for our own personal fulfilment but to
utilize them for the betterment and benefit of others –
such a personal choice cannot be conferred by others or
be derived from some external source, it must come from
within. Your fate and future must be crafted and designed
by you because such actions will actualize your autonomy,
and sovereignty and ultimately undergird and cement
your independence. The Rev. Dr. Martin Luther King, Jr.
likens it to having a blueprint for the construction of one's
life. He asked rhetorically "what is your life's blueprint?
He then elaborated, "whenever a building is constructed,
you usually have an architect who draws a blueprint. Now

each of you is in the process of building the structure of your lives, and the question is whether you have a proper, a solid and a sound blueprint". In essence, Dr. King is challenging us that making decisions about our careers cannot be left to chance, ambivalence or even ambiguity. It is imperative that we have an architectural plan for the building of our lives.

The noted poet and influential painter, Pablo Picasso, is even more pointed and precise in challenging us that it is not only important to discover our gift, or talent but to use them for a cause which extends beyond one's personal comfort. "The meaning of life is to find your gift and the purpose of life, is to give it away." Picasso asserts that the sharing of one's talent for the welfare and wellbeing of others lends purpose to life. Indeed without purpose a life is basically empty and bereft of fulfilment and satisfaction.

Kenneth Hildebrand, the author of many books such as "Achieving Real Happiness" eloquently explains the importance of finding a purpose in life by asserting that a life without purpose is wasted. "Multitudes of people drifting aimlessly to and fro without a set purpose, deny themselves such fulfilment of their capacities and the satisfying happiness which attends it. They are not wicked they are only shallow, or they are not mean or vicious, they simply are empty…without purpose, their lives ultimately wander into a morass of dissatisfaction". A life without purpose or meaning can leave one emotionally void and vacuous. Ayn Rand is even more extreme in articulating his agreement "To me there is only one form of human depravity – the man without a purpose".

I would like to share this advice and warning specifically to young persons who are in the process of preparing to make educational, professional and career choices that will eventually shape their social and emotional profile. In my professional life, both as a clergyman and a college professor, I was fortunate for the opportunity to interact with many young people who were struggling to make these profound choices for their lives. Central to their concern were the quintessential questions - what do I want to become? what path should I pursue that will be personally sustaining, fulfilling and enriching while allowing me to contribute to the greater good of the society? These are very difficult choices and there are many pitfalls that can frustrate the road map that many have used to accomplish their goals and realized their dreams. Your youthfulness can be your greatest asset in that it can provide you with the promise and opportunities that invariably are endemic to this stage of your development. On the other hand it can become your greatest liability if you fallaciously embraced the view that youthfulness provides you with an inordinate and unlimited amount of time to make a more decisive choice. This is but a recipe for procrastination. Lacking in focus you stand in danger of missing critical opportunities for progress. Unfortunately, this can lead to the depth of frustration which can either delay one's goals or in the worst scenario or alternative abandon one's dreams.

It is therefore important that one should be focused and be tenacious in trying to refine and define one's aspirations with the precision that will make them realistic and achievable. History has provided us with the exhortation of many great writers and thinkers who have warned us about the grave consequences of the failure to use time wisely and in a judicious and prudent manner. The 18th century poet Edward Young, warns us that anyone who has a tendency to postpone, delay and put off things generally achieves little. "procrastination is the thief of time" The English poet and author Geoffrey Chaucer proclaimed that "tide and time wait for no one". The ancient Latin phrase "tempus fugit" which means time flies is more than a subtle warning that we should be vigilant stewards of time. The underlying motif in all of these famous sayings is the irrefutable fact that time lost can never be retrieved.

Another grave misstep which some students tend to make is equating a career with a hobby. A hobby is an activity which you may engage in periodically, intermittently or spasmodically when you feel like it. A career provides for your livelihood. To express it in a more down to earth manner - a career enables you to put food on the table.

Finally, a career choice that is exclusively confined to putting food on the table "that is merely satisfying our social, physical and material needs will fall short of providing you with the inner satisfaction that will give your life a sense of purpose, meaning and mission. One can find a tremendous sense of fulfilment with the knowledge and feeling that one is contributing to a cause that is greater than oneself.

As you begin to formulate and forge a blueprint for your life you should consider this as a time of discernment in which you will seek and search for the input of others. Avail yourself of the input, experience and expertise of others such as guidance counselors and career advisors. In addition, listen to your inner voice which invariably defines your dreams. The failure to be focused on this aspect of our life can lead to a sense of inadequacy and uselessness, unlike Mr. Frank Sinatra, your regrets will not be few – they will be many, myriad and manifold.

CHAPTER 8

EDUCATION AND IT'S IMPORTANCE

———◦❈◦———

"Education is the most powerful weapon that
can change the world" Nelson Mandela

There can be no doubt that as we begin to assemble our lives and make preparation to build our future, that we should be cognizant of the pivotal role which education can play in bringing these goals to fruition. In fact, it is not an overstatement to conclude that education is indispensable to any degree of human success. It is an integral part of the foundation upon which all our dreams, goals and aspirations are realized. Education is an investment that can yield dividends that will equip and enable us to confront, cope and control the complex environment in which we find ourselves. It helps us to better control the circumstances and complex conditions of life. It can be the tool in shaping and building one's life.

Ironically, while education can be used as a tool to advance one's hopes and dreams, historically it has been used as a weapon in some societies, to stratify people, to degrade, devalue, dehumanize and ultimately destroy them. In some societies, education was a privilege reserved for the few. Access to education was confined only to those who were destined to become the ruling class. Such a system regulated and determined one's status in life while consigning and restricting others to subordinate and subservient roles. This system and custom conferred to one group, the right, the power and the authority to determine who should be denied access to education. The ultimate tragedy of such injustice was the fact that education became the preeminent instrument of the oppression of many while creating a permanent system of brutal inequality.

The most severe and compelling example of education being used as a weapon to destroy others was its use to perpetuate, prolong and preserve the institution of slavery by depriving the enslaved access to any kind of formal education. It was the most powerful weapon of control. This policy was enacted into legislation and encoded into the hearts and habits of others particularly in places like the United States of America. It was designed particularly to keep slaves in ignorance. It was widely believed and articulated that literacy would awaken a sense of discontent among the enslaved. It would open their minds to think and open their eyes to a vision that they deserved a better future. The slave owners believed that literacy would embolden a sense of discontent among the slaves and foment a sense of rebellion to improve their plight. A prominent Washington lawyer Elias B. Caldwell expressed most graphically the strategy and fear of the slave owner. That literacy was antithetical to the institution of slavery and was therefore a threat to their livelihood. The following statement expressed their grave concerns "the more you improve the condition of these people, the more miserable you make them, in their present state. You give them a higher relish for those privileges which they can never attain and turn what we intend for a blessing [slavery] into a curse. No, if they must remain in their present situation, keep them in their present situation, keep them in the lowest state of degradation and ignorance. The nearer you bring them to the conditions of brutes, the better chance do you give them of possessing their apathy." The prominent ex-slave, social reformer, abolitionist and statesman Frederick Douglass expressed in his biography that he understood the pathway from slavery to freedom and it was to have the power to read and write. He asserted that once you learn to read you will be forever free. Furthermore, he affirmed that knowledge makes a man unfit to be a slave.

It is clear that no individual as well as no society can survive with any degree of productivity, prosperity and stability without a radical change in access to education. Education could no longer be a privilege reserved for the few but a human right that provided public and universal education for the entire populace. It was an old testament prophet who proclaimed that ignorance was responsible for the destruction of his community. He said, "my people are destroyed for lack of knowledge." The greatest threat to the welfare and wellbeing of any society is the pervasiveness and prevalence of ignorance. The prophet believed that his people, his community were ignorant of the law that provided guidance for healthy and productive living. It was their willful ignorance and failure to learn the fundamental tenets and principles of the law that led to their destruction. In essence it was their ignorance that destroyed them.

It was the awareness of the lethal nature of ignorance coupled with the gross inequities which it engendered that spawned the movement for the establishment of public education. In this context education would be a right for all and not a privilege for the few. This was the philosophy embraced and executed by Horace Mann, the pioneer and father of public education in Boston, Massachusetts. This was a most radical idea of his time in that it removed education from the private and privileged domain into the public arena thereby giving access to all those who were excluded. Horace Mann's rationale behind his novel and bold proposal was that public education would be the great "equalizer". According to Mann public education would be the harbinger of equality. It would afford the under-privileged and the disadvantaged the opportunity to become equal with others. He contended that education would empower those at the lower level of the social ladder to ascend and advance to it uppermost round. This promise would not be manipulated by the mandates of others but would be accessible to all. It would only be contingent upon all those who are willing to climb.

This universal access to education would have its impact not only on the individual but would redound to the enrichment of the wider community. In his famous address entitled, "The necessity for education in a republic", Mann forcefully and emphatically opined that "in a republic ignorance is a crime." It is demonstrably clear that the benefits of education are not only multidimensional in nature but inestimable as well. The first by-product of being educated is that it is liberating. Frederick Douglass not only saw the nexus between literacy and education, he experienced it and he expressed it with deep conviction, "if you learn to read you are forever free". The slave owner on the other hand recognized that the slaves' mere exposure to literacy and education in any form would emancipate them from the darkness of ignorance. The deprivation of education was the most powerful weapon used to control the enslaved and reduced them to brutes, "undeserving of the privileges which they can never attain."

The second by product and benefit of education is the fact that it is empowering. It can be the source of power for those who embrace it. This point of view was poignantly articulated by the noted British statesman and philosopher Sir Francis Bacon who in his treatise "scientia potentia est" asserted that "knowledge is power". Knowledge endows one with the power to think and this ability to think validates ones very existence. "I think therefore I am" is attributed to the French philosopher René Descartes and according to him it allows you to know yourself and to discover yourself esteem. It's enabling, in that it lays the foundation for self-affirmation and self-advocacy. It empowers you to uphold your sovereignty, safeguard your independence and defend your dignity, thereby validating your self-worth.

The third dimension and by-product of education is its transformative nature. It can produce change because it opens doors, eyes and minds. Every former slave who gained access to education can bear witness to this mental and emotional conversion. The late President and great leader of South Africa Nelson Mandela is credited with making this profound observation. "Education is the most powerful weapon which you can use to change the world" Nelson Mandela was part of a nation that was governed by apartheid. Apartheid was entrenched in the institutions of that society with virtually no hope of any change. Yet many like Mandela shared the vision that what seemed impossible was possible. Education not only gave them the vision and insight to dream of a better day, but it equipped them with the requisite resources to actualize it.

At this point I would like to focus my attention on the youth and the importance of education. Most of you are in the midst of making choices or you are on the threshold of making choices about your educational path, this is without doubt one of the most critical and consequential choices which you can make for your future. Education is too important to be relegated to a secondary role in your lives. You cannot be casual or cavalier about deciding what role it will play in the shaping and molding of your life. It is vitally important for you to appreciate the pivotal and preeminent role which education can play in the construction of your lives.

Education is without doubt an investment in yourselves so that you can compete in the marketplace of opportunities and promise. If you invest in yourselves it can yield many dividends that will equip you with the power to become productive individuals.

Failure to comprehend the importance of education and to seize the opportunities which it provides can only leave you with deficits which will either place you at a grave disadvantage or will render you dysfunctional. In the process you will devalue and short-change yourselves and most definitely become partners and participants in your own destruction. In essence, when you become an instrument in your own demise this is tantamount to emotional suicide-you kill your real potential, promise and power. The consequences of this is that in the marketplace of opportunity you unwittingly relegate yourselves as beggars, relying on others for favors rather than being able to trade and compete on an equal basis with others. You disadvantaged yourselves and forfeit the power which education, "the great equalizer" would have given you.

Education is not simply the means which provides you with the skills that are necessary to obtain a job or a career. Though this is an important component, it is more comprehensive than that. In its totality education enables you to become a whole, complete and productive person.

CHAPTER 9

CHARACTER IS YOUR ROAD MAP

———⋙◆⋘———

"Among the many things that will destroy us most is knowledge without character." Mahatma Ghandi

In Chapter 8, I described the critical role which education can play in the formation of a person's life and the execution and accomplishment of one's mission. It is accepted by prominent thinkers and researchers that the benefits of education are manifold. Education can be liberating, empowering and transforming and its impact on a person's life is demonstrably formidable and consequential. But education, though important is only one facet of the requirements that are necessary for living and experiencing a holistic and complete life. In short, while education will place a person on a trajectory for a meaningful and successful life, it is but one component in a person's tool kit. In essence, education alone will not be adequate to meet the needs of a person's growth and development, it is but one device in an individual's arsenal for maintaining and improving one's quality of life.

Mahatma Ghandi, the renowned leader in a very

compelling statement, warned us that among the many things that can destroy a person is when a person possesses knowledge without character. He listed a compendium of the things that can destroy us and he identified knowledge without character as one of the leading factors that will destroy us. "The things that will destroy us are politics without principle, pleasure without conscience, wealth without work, knowledge without character, business without morality, science without humanity and worship without sacrifice". An American educator, author and businessman ... elaborating on Ghandi's analysis went even further to underscore the fact that the consequences of knowledge without character are not only serious but severe. He remarked, "As dangerous as a little knowledge is, even more dangerous is much knowledge without a strong principled character. Purely intellectual development without commensurate internal character makes as much sense as putting a high-powered sports car in the hands of a teenager on drugs". The Apostle Paul, writing to a community at the city of Corinth, made the observation that knowledge without a moral compass will yield nothing to our stature "Though I have all knowledge ... without love I gain nothing". He further contended that knowledge is not infinite, "as for knowledge it will end." Knowledge then is not a permanent feature of one's personality, it is limited in its duration.

Character on the other hand is enduring. It is a permanent feature of our being which no one can take away from us. Abraham Lincoln, addressing the permanency of character, drew the distinction between character and reputation. He said that character is like a tree and reputation is like its shadow. One has roots and is immovable, the other is fleeting and transitory. "Character is like a tree and reputation like a shadow. The shadow is what we think of it, but the tree is the real thing. Character is what one has, but reputation is what others think one has". The noted Greek Philosopher, Heraclitus, has been credited with the aphorism that "character is destiny". The implication here is the acknowledgement that a person's future or even fate is not determined by external forces but by the values and virtues which we cultivate and possess in our lives, that each individual is in charge of his or her destiny. Where we eventually end up will be determined by our actions; and our actions, for the most part are shaped by the values of our character. In Shakespeare's Julius Caesar, Cassius is debating with Brutus about why some people remain in subordinate status rather than progressing to the status of nobility. He contended that this was not due to any external force but was due to their own inaction. "The fault dear Brutus, is not in our stars but in ourselves. That we are underlings."

When we speak about destiny, it can be defined in very

simple terms as reaching the place where a person intends to go in life. It is the successful fulfilment of the goals and purpose which one has crafted for him or herself. What an individual wants to become and what he or she wants to accomplish in life are integral parts of the defining characteristics of destiny. The fulfilment of one's dreams has interchangeably been referred to as self-realization or self-actualization. It is the fulfilment of one's maximum potential. This self-realization, the achievement of one's destiny is contingent upon the nature and quality of one's character. Character is the repository of the aggregate of the values and principle which drive, direct, motivate or guide a person's actions. These attributes of character can invariably determine or influence one's success or failure or one's happiness or one's sense of disappointment. The content of our character can bring us to what Erik Erikson, the social Psychologist, describes as one of two states or stages. Integrity or despair. The state of integrity is the experience of satisfaction with one's life, the state of despair is the guilt which comes from missed opportunities and failure.

The traits and attributes are varied and many. Among them are honesty, respect, courage, fairness, loyalty, perseverance and many others. Let us take the attribute of perseverance and the role it can play in a person's advancement in life. My kindergarten teacher would constantly encourage all of us in his class with the words that are now permanently etched in my mind. "If at first you don't succeed try and try again" or as my mother would incessantly remind me that perseverance seldom fails. In almost all of our endeavors, the ability to endure and not to retreat, the capacity to persevere and not to succumb to frustration are critical in helping us to avoid failure and defeat. Perseverance comes from falling or failing and getting back up. It is this conviction coupled with action that will build resilience. With this mindset, failure will be viewed as a lesson and not as a setback. Closely aligned with the critical attribute of perseverance is an equally important component of our character – attitude. In fact, it is virtually beyond contradiction that our attitude influences everything we say or do. One prominent writer expresses it in very colorful language. "Attitude is your paintbrush it colors everything." If our attitude allows us to sow the seeds of negativity, we can expect that we will reap the crop of failure and frustration. On the other hand, if our attitude allows us to approach life with a sense of positivity then hope and optimism will be the driving force behind our actions. Our attitude may very well determine the altitude which we reach in life. The capacity to love is perhaps the definitive attribute that is a prerequisite for a sound and stable character. It is the trust which lays the foundation for empathy, compassion and respect for others. It is the love that helps us to build healthy relationships that are vital for social interaction, collegiality and personal advancement. Genuine love allows us to manage and conquer the egocentric tendencies that are inimical to human fellowship, it enables us to sublimate and keep in check the selfish proclivities which constantly threaten the experience of social cohesion which produces peace of mind and harmony.

In conclusion, your reputation is temporary, transitory and fleeting – subject to the whims of others who can defile, deface or even destroy it. On the other hand, your character is, and can be, a permanent feature of your being because you are the sole custodian and steward of it. No one can take it away from you without your permission. Like the soul, your essence is inviolate, no one can take it away from you because it lies deep within the core of your being. The great singer, Whitney Houston, left us an immutable message. Her song conveys that there are certain things which people can't plunder or steal. Our pride, our love and above all our dignity because they reside in the reservoir of our souls. "...they can't take away my dignity...I found the greatest love of all inside of me ..." because it resides in the recesses of my soul. Your character and your destiny are primarily in your hands.

CHAPTER 10

FORGIVENESS

———⟶⊰●⊱⟵———

"It's one of the greatest gifts you can give yourself to forgive, forgive everybody" Maya Angelou

It is noteworthy that the concept of forgiveness is not listed among the traditional cardinal virtues which represent the foundation of national morality nor is it discussed in any detailed form in much of the literature in psychology and other disciplines which deal with human behavior. Yet I believe strongly that forgiveness is essential and paramount for human growth, progress, survival and security. While forgiveness is found in the major religions of the world and figures prominently in their teachings, it is not exclusively a religious tenet and dogma. Indeed, many have either fallaciously dismissed it as being irrelevant to their needs or have relegated it to a low priority in their lives because they have confined its relevance primarily to people of religious faith. Many perceive it as exclusively a religious phenomenon.

However, when we move from a superficial analysis, or a mere casual or cosmetic assessment of its meaning and value, to a deeper examination of its role and purpose in human affairs, we discover that forgiveness is critical not only for personal sanity, emotions, health and wholeness but also for the building and preservation of a strong, stable and viable community. It is not an exaggeration to conclude that forgiveness is the cornerstone for community building. In fact, it is the intrinsic ethos of the community.

Among the major religions the practice of forgiveness is directly related and associated with the realization and preservation of the community. In Judaism, its practice is not simply a preference or option, it is not a voluntary act but a duty. Yom Kippur, or the day of the atonement, is one of the most important observance of the Jewish calendar. It is a common obligation. In Islamic teachings forgiveness which is more commonly referred to as pardon is prevalent in several verses of the Koran in which Muslims are strongly encouraged to forgive wrongdoing. In Christianity forgiveness stands at the apex of its teachings. Indeed, forgiveness may rightly be classified as the raison d'etre of its mission. The roots of forgiveness can be traced to God's attempt to forgive human sin and shortcomings and to set in motion the emergence of a new community which would be sustained by persons forgiving each other. Forgiveness then permeates the teachings and content of Christian thinking, theology and philosophy because it maintains the bond that is vital for the life of the community. It's the glue that keeps the new community viable.

To underscore the importance of forgiveness, Jesus in the Lord's prayer equates the importance of forgiveness with the importance of food for the nourishment of the body, one cannot live without them. "Give us this day our daily bread and forgive us our sins as we forgive those who sin against us." Just as food is indispensable to the sustainability of the body, forgiveness is an imperative for the life and durability of the community. Living in, and being part of, a community automatically means that interpersonal relationships and the quality of those relationships are indispensable to the future and survival of that community. This inevitably means that when relationships are fractious because of human frailty and fallibility there must be a mechanism of repairing, restoring and renewing those fractures and fissures. This can only be achieved and be realized through the process of forgiveness, pardon and atonement. Forgiveness maintains the bond which enables the individual to realize his fullest potential. All of us are diminished when we live in isolation and estrangement from each other. All human life is interconnected. For good or ill we cannot live independently from each other. The 17th century English poet John Donne expresses it in one of his most famous writings. "No man is an island entire of itself.

Every man is a piece of the continent, a part of the main. If a clod be washed away by the sea, Europe is the less, as well as if a promontory were as well as any manor of thy friends or of thine own were; any one's death diminishes me because I am involved in mankind." The Rev. Dr. Martin Luther King, Jr. expresses this interconnectedness and interdependence in equally compelling terms, "We are all caught in an inescapable network of mutuality, tied together in a single garment of destiny, whatever affects one directly affects all indirectly". On another occasion, he expresses this consideration in even more colorful language. The initial choice before us is that "we must either learn to live as brothers or we shall perish as fools".

The adage "to err is human to love is divine" is the acknowledgement that all human beings are fallible. Fallibility is an intrinsic part of human nature. This means that sooner rather than later we will offend, harm and hurt each other. Both in word and in deed, all of us will commit acts that will be injurious and inimical to a whole and healthy community. All of us are indebted to each other and must be engaged in a constant and continuous effort to repair and restore the fractured and broken nature of our community. Such restoration and renewal can only be accomplished through the radical practice of forgiveness.

Both in sacred and secular circles there is the almost

universal recognition of the need to practice forgiveness. We may use different synonyms to describe or define forgiveness but the need to mend broken relationships is a prerequisite for social order and personal emotional equilibrium. The alternative couldn't be more precarious. The failure to forgive or the unwillingness to forgive can lead to chaos and disorder in the body politic. Forgiveness is not easy to practice. It is a difficult task which demands considerable effort from each one of us. There is a tendency by many that the call to forgive is a one-sided affair which demands forgiveness by some and not by others. There is always the false assumption that we are the donor and dispenser of forgiveness rather than being the recipients and beneficiaries of the forgiveness of others whom we have offended. However, all of us have benefitted from the forgiveness and understanding of others throughout our lives. We have benefitted from the forgiveness of our parents, our peers, our friends, families our neighbors, our colleagues and even strangers. All of whom we have offended in word, action or inaction. In biblical literature there is the implication that it becomes easier to forgive others when we acknowledge that we have been forgiven by others.

In Jesus' familiar sermon on the mount in which he articulated the very substance and essence of Christian ethical and moral behavior, he expended and appropriated a great deal of time on the imperative of forgiveness. Many have criticized Jesus' call for radical forgiveness as being extreme, hyperbolic, naïve, impractical, utopian and above all unrealistic. However, Jesus knew of the destructive, devasting and deadly nature of the alternative which is revenge, retaliation and retribution. Revenge is not a symptom or side effect, it is the disease itself, it is a pathogen of the human heart. Revenge is the progenitor of hatred and not the love which can facilitate and enable us with the capacity to forgive. "You have heard that it was said "an eye for an eye and a tooth for a tooth" but I say unto to you, do not resist an evil doer. But if anyone strikes you on the right cheek turn the other side also." Many tend to dismiss this advice of Jesus as being fool hardy, but Jesus knew of the deadly consequences of retaliation which would inevitably lead us into a protracted and prolonged war with our enemy. This prolonged situation will induce the kind of stress that will be forever our constant companion. Indeed, it will cheat us of the experience of peace and tranquility in our lives. It was the noted Prime Minister of the United Kingdom, Sir Winston Churchill, who opined that revenge is always counterproductive. "Revenge is of all satisfactions the most costly and long drawn out, retributive persecution is of all policies, the most pernicious". Sir Winston Churchill is correct in conceding that the pursuit of revenge is both costly and interminable. The additional pain which comes from turning the other cheek is not only considerably less painful, but it is short lived. Above all, it prevents one from being engaged in a long and protracted struggle consumed with incessant anger. Many others who find difficulty in accepting Jesus' call to turn the other cheek see it as a cowardly act of surrender and certainly a symbol of weakness. However, we are reminded by the renowned civil rights leader of India who opined that forgiveness is the attribute of the strong. "The weak can never forgive, forgiveness is the attribute of the strong". Forgiveness is not only a duty towards each other, it is a strategy that liberates us from the imprisonment of hatred. Lewis B. Smedes an ethicist and theologian said, "to forgive is to set a prisoner free and discover that the prisoner is you". The person who forgives benefits as much as the person who is forgiven. According to Smedes, it is a liberation from the demonic forces of anger and bitterness that held us captive and deprive us of the ability to love even our enemies. There is an anonymous saying that "when you choose to forgive those who hurt you, you take away their power". When Maya Angelou said that "forgiveness is the greatest gift you can give yourself…" hence we should forgive everybody. She was affirming that forgiveness can free us and purge us from the toxins which contaminate our hearts.

A heart that is polluted, with anger, hatred, malice and revenge is a heart that is deprived of the blessings of life. "Blessed are the pure in heart for they shall see God." In one of his letters to a Christian community the Apostle Paul exhorted his people not to delay or postpone addressing anger. "Let not the sun set on your anger." I interpret that to mean that we should never take anger to bed with us. Settle your differences quickly. Taking anger to bed is tantamount to building a close, cozy and intimate relationship with anger which can only destroy your ability to forge meaningful relationships with anyone. Do not let anger share such an intimate experience with you. Anger breeds hatred and hatred annihilates the ability to forgive.

One does not have to be a religious person to understand the compelling need for forgiveness. Religion may be the most potent source in the advocacy of forgiveness. Nevertheless, in the secular phases of our lives we will discover that repairing broken relationships, healing the wounds of estrangement and enmity require forgiveness which is the balm that makes the wounded whole.

CHAPTER 11

GREED

⟶⊷⊶⟵

"Earth provides enough to satisfy everyman's needs but not every man's greed" Mahatma Ghandi

Earlier I asserted that as a person attempts to construct and assemble his or her life that there are certain values and attributes of character that anyone should possess in order to be successful in life. These values and attributes are the building blocks that will help to ensure that a person reaches his or her maximum potential. These building blocks form the foundation of the structure of one's life and will enable a person to achieve a sense of wholeness, strength and fulfilment. For instance, the quality of a person's character can shape and determine the trajectory of one's life and the pursuit of education can play a dominate role in the realization of one's dreams. This lends credence to the familiar maxims that character is destiny and knowledge is power.

There are certain values that we must strive to possess, embrace and uphold if we are to achieve any significant measure of success and happiness. These are all part and parcel of the material of the building blocks that will become the cornerstone of one's destiny. However, any attempt in the pursuit of happiness, success and fulfilment must be accompanied by an acute awareness of those factors that run counter to these goals and are antithetical to such ambitions. Preeminent among these factors that militate against one's quest for happiness is greed. Indeed, greed can be such a destructive force in an individual's life, that it has been listed among the "seven deadly sins". Deadly is perhaps the most appropriate ascription because greed can derail, doom and ultimately destroy an individual's life and sense of happiness. Among the many definitions of greed, there is a common thread that is present and pervasive in all of them, that greed is an excessive desire for more, specifically for wealth, power, possessions and prestige.

The excessive desire for more material things deludes a person into thinking that the acquisition and accumulation of these things will be a guarantor of one's success and happiness. Tragically, this excessive desire is intrinsically insatiable, and it can entrap a person into an endless quest which thirst cannot be quenched. The prominent psychologist Eric Fromm in his book "Escape from Freedom" expresses it more succinctly. "Greed is a bottomless pit which exhausts a person in an endless effort to satisfy the need without reaching satisfaction." The Roman poet and satirist, Quintas Horace Flaccas, has noted that "the covetous man is ever in want". Seneca reminds us that for "greed all nature is too little" and coupled with this he opined that "it is not the man who has little, but he who desires more that is poor."

The first consequence of greed is the fact that those who have become its captives are consumed with an endless and incessant desire for possessions that will not produce satisfaction or contentment. Moreover, these things for which we passionately yearn are not enduring, they are transitory and ephemeral. There is a biblical admonition that stipulates that those things which we treasure most, material things, power and possessions can be withdrawn, confiscated and withheld or be stolen. They are not permanent features of our lives in that we can lose them in some form or another. "Do not store up for yourselves treasures on earth, where moth and rust corrupt and where thieves break in and steal." It's a dire warning that power and possessions are expendable and if they are the only things which define and direct our lives, then sooner or later we will be found wanting. We are reminded that as life brings its inevitable changes there will come a time when the limitations of material things will be exposed. Time will prove to us that their value to us is short lived. However, while possessions are perishable and power can be disposable, the most ominous and indeed sobering reality of human beings is that we are all mortals. The Rev. Dr. Martin Luther King, Jr. refers to this phenomenon as "that experience which is the irreducible common denominator of all men, death". One of the certainties of human existence is that we are all terminal and come into the world with an expiration date. It is the great equalizer of all people.

When greed, the lust for power, the excessive desire to accumulate possessions, the propensity to hoard anything which we can touch are viewed in this context, then those who are captives of greed, those who have fallen prey to its innocuous spell will discover that it is all vanity. We have to leave everything behind. There is a biblical story concerning a man called Job. He experienced considerable loss, his livelihood, his business, his children and a massive deterioration in his health. These tragic circumstances brought him to a place to realize loss and its experience with a broader perspective. He came to the realization that those things which he valued as dear, his business, his children and even his life, were all transitory, temporary and fleeting. They all have an expiration date and moreover, all of us have to leave our possessions, in whatever form they come, behind us. "Naked came I into this world from my mother's womb and naked I will return there". In another biblical story, the Apostle Paul, the elder statesman and mentor of young Timothy, is giving him some advice about how to manage his life and conduct himself as a leader. He charged Timothy to avoid the love of money because it is the root of evil. Paul knew that there was always the temptation to use life's opportunities to acquire material possessions. He knew of the fallacious belief that they could provide personal security and satisfaction. Paul also knew that in the end they would fail to provide both. Man cannot live by bread alone. Material possessions alone cannot sustain us but most importantly Paul reminded him that ultimately whatever we accumulate here on earth we have to leave it behind. His warning to Timothy was terse and unambiguous. "For we brought nothing into this world and it is certain that we can take nothing out." One Baptist preacher expressed this biblical tenet in more colorful language when he said I have never seen a cargo van attached to a hearse. In essence, no matter how much we accumulate in this life, we have to leave it behind. We cannot carry it with us to the grave. There is a story told by Jesus that poignantly illustrates the folly of those who rely on material goods to bring happiness, ease and contentment to their lives. Jesus tells the story of a very rich man who had become so successful that after hoarding all of his material possessions he discovered that he had no room to store his goods. However, the man eventually devised an elaborate scheme to expand his storage space and provide more room to hoard his belongings and that this would guarantee that he would be liberated from want and fear of deprivation. He believed that this shrewd action of his would redound to his attainment of happiness and success. But despite his success and his elaborate plans, Jesus called him a fool. This was language that was uncharacteristic of Jesus. Jesus employed that term to highlight the misguided thinking of this man. This man's actions exhibited the folly that equated the accumulation of wealth with the accomplishment of contentment. Jesus pointed him to the hollowness and emptiness of his plan. "This night thy soul is required of thee and the things which you prize who will inherit them?" The ultimate verdict rendered by Jesus was designed to educate, both this man and all others possessed with the flawed thinking, that eventually they would die and may not even know the beneficiary of their success and riches. The Rev. Dr. Martin Luther King, Jr., commenting on the story of the rich man, remarked that the man, having been duped by the emptiness of the abundance of material things, had died spiritually and emotionally even before his natural death. "After this man had accumulated his vast resources of wealth – at the moment when his stocks were accruing the greatest interest and his palatial home was the talk of the town – he came to that experience which is the irreducible common denominator of all men, death … Even if he had not died physically, he was already dead spiritually."

There is a striking correlation between greed being classified as a deadly sin and the Rev. Dr. King's contention that the greed of the rich fool inexorably led him to an emotional and spiritual death long before his natural and spiritual death. This viewpoint is reminiscent of a Shakespearian saying in Julius Caesar about cowardice which induces an experience of death that precedes physical death. "Cowards die many times before their death, the valiant only taste of death but once." I believe that the greedy person shares a similar experience. The greedy person dies many times before their death, but the caring and compassionate person only tastes death but once. Greed then is much more than an excessive desire to hoard and accumulate things, it is truly a deadly sin, it is a deadly force and a veritable agent of death because it kills a person's humanity.

The death of one's humanity manifests itself in many ways. The casualty of this moral and emotional death is the sense of compassion. The awareness of our duty to be concerned with the well-being of others. It is replaced by chronic selfishness and unchecked egocentric behavior. The greedy person is totally insensitive and oblivious to the needs, suffering and plight of others, it blunts one's senses of caring and blurs one's vision to the predicament of others. In fact, selfishness is almost synonymous with greediness. Secondly, and perhaps most ominous and lethal, greed destroys all forms and opportunities for building healthy and meaningful relationships. For the greedy person, every prospective relationship is viewed as an opportunity for rivalry and it reduces life and living to an ongoing competition. According to Professor Henri J. M. Nouwen, this competition is inculcated in us from a very early age. "Aren't we always asking ourselves whether we are better or worse, stronger or weaker, faster or slower than the one who stands beside us. Haven't we, from elementary school on, experienced most of our fellow human beings as rivals in the quest for success, influence, and popularity?" When life becomes an ongoing competition, then the most tragic consequence of this thinking is that our relationships are based upon rivalry. When there is no apparent competitor, the greedy person competes with himself and that is the quintessential recipe for self-destruction. Competing against oneself leaves no room to temper or tame one's unchecked desire for more. Bhagavad Gita has said that there are three gates which lead to self-destructive hell - lust, anger and greed.

The greedy person is grounded by a philosophy of not only 'keeping up with the Joneses' but surpassing and defeating them. Consequently, envy, jealousy and enmity are many of its by-products. If the love of money is the root of all evil, then greed is the seed from which all evil germinates. Greed alienates people from each other, it builds a chasm between people and people. It is important to note that what prompted Jesus to tell the story of the rich fool and his greed was due to the occasion of one of two siblings imploring Jesus to settle a dispute among them concerning an inheritance which their father had left them. The rift and rivalry were so intense and divisive that their bond of brotherhood became secondary. The lust for the material resources of the inheritance defined their relationship. It was non-existent, it was dead.

The noted political activist Velupillai Prabhakaran in his fight for equality, is credited with stating that "All human suffering springs from unbridled desire, unless one extricates oneself from the clutch of greed one will not free himself from the fetters of sorrow." Greed ensnares us in the fetters of sorrow. It is a gateway to self-destructive hell but above all it is the agent of death – greed can kill you.

CHAPTER 12

GRATITUDE

"Gratitude is not only the greatest of all virtues, but the parent of others."
Marcus Tullus Cicero
Never forget to say thank you.

I f there is one thing that I can remember from my infancy it is the actions of my parents, particularly my mother who consistently encouraged me to say 'thank you' to anyone who gave me something or offered me assistance of any kind. As I grew older they would instill in me either by word or example the importance of expressing gratitude. "Don't forget to say thank you", was a familiar charge in our home. I am sure that this was a practice that was not unique to our household, it was not only prevalent in my home. Indeed, it was buttressed by other socializing institutions. It was taught in the school and was imparted to us in the religious instructions of the church. Whenever we were reminded to say thank you or reprimanded for not doing so we were told that saying thank you was simply good manners.

A few years ago I was very surprised that the President

of Yale University, Peter Salovey, chose gratitude as the theme for his Baccalaureate address to Yale's graduating class of 2014 – the importance of saying thank you. The President applauded the graduates for reaching this personal achievement but simultaneously reminded them that they could not have reached this significant milestone without the help of many players, from their parents, professors to the janitors. They owed a debt of gratitude to all who made this day possible. It may be that the parental instinct of the president might have influenced his choice of gratitude as his theme and topic. My surprise at Mr. Salovey's choice of this theme stemmed from the fact that it was somewhat out of character with similar addresses to graduating classes. Generally, the highlight of such addresses tends to focus almost exclusively on the success of the students and how this moment will equip them to capitalize on and cope with the challenges which await them. Success, opportunities and promise tend to be the natural corollaries of graduation. Realizing their dreams while helping to enrich the lives of others tend to figure prominently on occasions such as these. Yet, as those students reached such a pinnacle of success, the president chose a more sobering, subdued and humbling topic – gratitude. However, he was quick to stress that the expression of gratitude is much more than being socially polite or as my parents called it, "good manners". Rather, according to the president, gratitude is a "core human capacity".

Gratitude then is recognized as a most potent emotional force that is vital for healthy living both for the benefit of the individual as well as the community. It cannot be stressed enough that it is much more than being polite or just practicing good manners. In almost every culture and religion, there are rituals and ceremonies that provide opportunities for individuals as well as the community to express gratitude in various forms. In Jewish circles, The Feast of the Harvest also called The Feast of the First Fruits, Israelites were exhorted collectively to offer the fruits of the harvest to God as an expression of gratitude to God for making the harvest possible. In many of the Jewish writings such as the Book of Psalms, individuals expressed their gratitude to God for the benefits which they have received from Him and with a corresponding pledge never to forget, "Bless the Lord, O my soul and forget not all His benefits". It was a similar conviction that motivated and prompted President Abraham Lincoln to issue a proclamation in 1860 making provision for a national day of Thanksgiving. The proclamation read in part "to set apart and observe the last Thursday of November as a day of thanksgiving and praise to our beneficent Father who dwelleth in the heavens". Both in sacred and secular writings gratitude has been exalted as a virtue which we should embrace because it can enrich our lives both individually and collectively. Several thinkers and philosophers have written about the importance of gratitude, many urging that we should strive to own it and employ it whenever necessary and appropriate in our interactions with others. Marcus Tullus Cicero lauds gratitude as not only being the greatest of all virtues but the parent of others. Giving gratitude such a prominent place, Cicero implies that it gives birth to all other virtues. The renowned Swiss theologian Karl Barth, in stressing the importance of gratitude in our lives, contends that it can be the source of joy. The American poet, philosopher and Essayist Ralph Waldo Emerson, was a forceful proponent of encouraging others to develop gratitude as a permanent feature of their lives. "Cultivate the habit of being grateful for every good thing which comes to you and give thanks continuously. And because all things have contributed to your advancement, you should include all things in your gratitude."

The benefits of being grateful are multidimensional in nature. Gratitude helps both its donor as well as the recipient. This should dispel the notion that being grateful helps only the recipient. There are mutual benefits. One only has to look at the widely held definition gratitude, "Gratitude is a thankful appreciation of what an individual receives, whether tangible or intangible. With gratitude, people acknowledge the goodness in their lives. In the process, people usually recognize that the source of that goodness lies at least partially outside themselves." Gratitude not only celebrates our accomplishments, it simultaneously acknowledges the contribution of others to our success. Alfred North Whitehead, the 20th century British mathematician and philosopher, wholeheartedly supports such a viewpoint, "No one who achieves success does so without the help of others. The wise and confident acknowledge this help with gratitude". It is widely held that gratitude can boost one's mental and physical health and helps to build and foster healthier relationships. According to Yale President Dr Peter Salovey, gratitude is one of the keys to happiness. A study published by Harvard Medical School highlights the fact that happiness is a byproduct of gratitude. "Gratitude is strongly and consistently associated with greater happiness, it helps people feel most positive emotions, relish good experiences, improve their health, deal with adversity and building strong relationships. Gratitude is also credited with helping to build cohesiveness in communities and societies which have traditions and rituals designed to express thanksgiving in some form or another. On the other hand, the absence of gratitude in one's emotions tends to lead one into the territory of cynicism, pessimism and may engender many negative emotions. This leads to a feeling that one is impotent to deal with life's challenges. We can easily become preoccupied and fixated with failure, loss and the setback which come our way. Gratitude, however, allows us to refocus our attention on the balance sheet of our lives. When we pursue this positive path, we will discover that the profits are significantly more than the deficits.

There is a gospel song which succinctly captures this human dilemma. The author tells us that when we think that we have reached rock bottom, when we think that we have lost it all, rather than capitulate to cynicism and surrender to depression that we should return to the balance sheet of our life experiences. Where, rather than exaggerate our losses we will rediscover our gains and reclaim our blessings. Indeed, we will be astounded that life is good and worth living "When upon life's billows you are tempest tossed, when you are discouraged thinking all is lost, count you many blessings name them one by one and it will surprise you what the Lord has done". This is not just a pious platitude designed to placate and pacify those who are facing life's challenges and crises. Nor is it an attempt to discount or dismiss the gravity of our pain but it is an invitation to balance your experience by revisiting your gains. Let gratitude direct your thoughts and shape your attitude. I believe that all of us in such a situation, when we are discouraged thinking all is lost, we should apply this mathematical equation to our life experiences. Count your blessings rather than calculate your problems for the latter will only multiply your pain and subtract from your serenity. Be always willing and ready to say, "Thank You".

CHAPTER 13

DO NOT BE JUDGMENTAL

"The happiest people I have known are evaluating and improving themselves. The unhappy people are usually evaluating and judging others'" Plato

"Do not judge by appearances but judge with right judgement." John 7:24

I t is widely held that making judgements about others is a natural human instinct which has been with us since the beginning of time. Many have even conceded that it is a vital and necessary component of how we live. But to express it in simple terms there are judgements and there are judgements. There are some judgements which help us to make decisions about the many choices which we are required to make in life and then there are other judgements particularly when we make them about people that can be very harmful to the person being judged. Dr. Raj Raghunathan, renowned author and university professor, in an article "Don't be judgmental be discerning" draws a sharp distinction between two kinds of judging, being judgmental and being discerning. There is a qualitative difference between them. He contends that there is a judgement that is discerning which is achieved through introspection and there is a judgement that is potentially damning and is intrinsically judgmental because it is rooted in preconceived notions. In essence he asserts categorically how discerning is different from being judgmental. "Without the ability to discern one wouldn't be able to get through life. The ability to discern is fundamental to making decisions and decisions are what allows us to get through life."

However, being judgmental has the tendency to base one's judgement solely on inferences and preconceived biases that lead to the devaluation and dehumanization of others. Dr. Ray Raghunathan elaborates, "A judgmental person is precisely the kind to go beyond discerning differences in people's abilities to make inferences about their overall worthiness. To a judgmental person a bad singer is inferior not just on the dimension of singing but is inferior on the more fundamental dimension of being human as well." While judgement is a natural human instinct, we cannot base our judgement exclusively on instinct, intuition, inference or even ignorance. Judgements emanating from the former will always be flawed when they are devoid of empirical and factual evidence or if it is based upon superficial assessment of any kind. The propensity to be judgmental, the spontaneous and cavalier way in which we are quick to pass judgement on anyone is a phenomenon that can be harmful and injurious to both parties ~ he who judges and he who is being judged.

I should like to share a personal experience which illustrates succinctly the dangerous aspect of judging others based upon inference. Several decades ago there was a television personality who produced and anchored an extremely interesting and enlightening documentary on a weekly basis. Watching this program became a weekly routine for me. However, there was one misgiving about the program which increasingly made me uncomfortable, the television newsman was extremely overweight. As the program continued my interest shifted from its content to a fixation with the man's weight. My criticism of the man became more consistent and intense. I would ask myself and others why would he allow himself to gain so much weight and why was he failing to deal with this situation. I apportioned blame to this man based primarily upon watching his program without any knowledge of his situation. As we shall see later my criticism, my conclusions, my judgements were totally misplaced because they were bereft of any factual evidence. Subsequently, the program ended abruptly, and I later learned that the news personality had died. I made several enquiries about his death and I found a copy of his obituary which revealed that for many years he struggled with an auto immune disease which required the use of steroids as an important part of his treatment. This treatment severely increased his weight. The operative word here is "struggled". He fought and tried against the odds and he made every effort to control his weight but unfortunately it was beyond his control. I knew nothing about this man's situation and condition, yet I was assigning blame to him for failure to control his weight – he was either careless, gluttonous or both. My judgement was precipitous, premature and preconceived. Indeed, I failed to heed the warning that I should not judge by appearances but judge with right judgement that is rooted in facts. My unease which emanated from my misjudgment of this man robbed me of the opportunity to fully enjoy the program without being distracted by my limitations. Fortunately, he was untouched by my misjudgments. This experience is a demonstration that judgements made without context and without a factual basis are always flawed. This life experience taught me an everlasting lesson and rescued me from the well-earned and well-deserved guilt. Context is key whenever we think of judging others because it forces us to heed the warning in the old adage that we need to walk a mile in someone's shoes before judging anyone. It is easy to judge without recognizing that their situation is different from ours.

Another important issue which illustrates the danger of judging others is the fact that even with empirical evidence our judgement can be imperfect because as human beings we are all fallible. There is one anonymous saying that affirms this in very precise terms, "Judge me when you are perfect". The sobering reality of the human condition is the fact that our knowledge is limited, always incomplete, and our perception is indeed imperfect. The Apostle Paul was forced to address a situation in which a community was being fractured because of the flawed judgements that people were making of each other. In a letter to an early Christian community at Corinth, he warned the members of that community not to be quick to judge each other because their knowledge was partial, incomplete and their perception and vision were blurred. He told them "Now we know in part, now we see through a glass dimly". It is important to give the historical context of Paul's advice to gain some insight into his condemnation of the danger and damage of being judgmental and the attendant harmful consequences which it engenders. He was speaking to a Christian community which he founded and established. When he left that community to function independently, it became embroiled in divisiveness and dissention. These were based on ideological and philosophical grounds. The membership pledged their allegiances to various proponents of these philosophical differences. These differences produced many factions which led to bitterness and intolerance. What fueled and fed them were the judgements which they made of each other. Their intolerance was based upon making false judgements of each other. Paul's remedy for their situation was that they should embrace love, which is never judgmental because it fosters and contains the humility which allows them to know and acknowledge their limitations – "now we know in part", no matter how intelligent we become, our knowledge is partial and incomplete, therefore our judgement can never be perfect. "Now we see in a glass dimly", in other words, our vison is blurred, therefore, we can never have a panoramic view of the landscape of a person's actions and experiences to make a right judgement of that person. The noted and renowned author and theologian, William Barclay, writing about being judgmental and the damage and danger of judging others has opined "We never know the whole facts of the whole person ... The fact is that if we realized what some people go through, so far from condemning them we would be amazed that they have succeeded in being as good as they are".

Another negative consequence of judging others or being judgmental is the fact that it has been used by some as a tool to elevate oneself while degrading and denigrating the other person. It is the epitome of self-righteousness – I am better than the other person. In an article authored by Ella Alexander, entitled "The Age of Judgement", she opined that many people use judgmental behavior. The psychology behind judgmental behavior as a form of defense mechanism whereby they tend to deflect the attention of their shortcomings on to others. She claims that this intentionally puts the focus on others while projecting the appearance of moral superiority. According to Ms. Alexander, this practice gives a virtual boost to their self-image.

The unfortunate outcome of this tendency is the fact that when a person engages in evaluating and judging others that it simultaneously fails to address one's own inadequacies. This can lead to a feeling of being unfulfilled and a sense of unhappiness. This lends credence to the observation made by the Philosopher Plato, when he remarked, "The happiest people I have known are evaluating and improving themselves.

The unhappy people are usually evaluating and judging others". Judging others by standards which we never apply to ourselves is the quintessential definition of hypocrisy and it is another example of judgmental behavior that is very detrimental to others. This form of judgmental behavior is widely condemned and even more so in biblical literature. In the Sermon on the Mount, Jesus devoted considerable time condemning being judgmental because he knew that it was antithetical to community building and the preservation of the social order. "Do not judge others, in order that you may not be judged, for with the judgement with which you judge, you will be judged; and with the measure you measure to others, it will be measured to you. Why do you look for the speck of dust in your brother's eye? Or how will you say to your brother, let me remove the speck of dust from your eye, and see there is a plank in your own eye? Hypocrite! First remove the plank from your eye, then you will see clearly to remove the speck of dust from your brother's eye."

In conclusion, judging others is not simply a hypocritical act nor is it just a blatant act of raw self-righteousness. It cannot be dismissed as a benign and harmless condition. It can be lethal to those who are its victims. It can have a lasting impact on a person's self-esteem and have a paralyzing effect on their confidence. Many lives have been wrecked by the wrong judgements of others. History is replete with the wreckage of lives caused by the misjudgments of others. According to Professor William Barclay, "There is hardly anyone who has not been guilty of some grave misjudgment and there is hardly anyone who has not suffered from someone else's misjudgment". The harmful consequences of being judgmental is that it creates and perpetuates stereotypes that stigmatize others, it hurts and harms people, it berates and belittles people, it devalues and dehumanizes them. People are left to bear the burden of the misjudgments imposed upon them by others. It can also be a self-imposed burden on those who are quick to judge others because it obscures your own deficits and makes you blind to the plank that is in your own eye. All should heed the warning. Judge not.

CHAPTER 14

TAKING STOCK OF YOUR LIFE

"The unexamined life is not worth living" Socrates

Some years ago, I was in a shopping center, and as I contemplated entering a store, I recognized a notice which read "Store Closed for Stocktaking". Coincidentally, the manager of this store was near it's entrance and he politely said to me, "I am sorry this store will be closed for the next two days". As we engaged in a lighthearted conversation, he went on to elaborate and explain the purpose and basis for this yearly routine. He stressed that taking stock was an in-depth appraisal and thorough assessment of the merchandise and all other assets of the store in order to ensure the marketing and financial health of the business. He further emphasized that this was a very intensive process that included an itemized list and record of the resources of what was available in stock. Items that were in demand and were selling quickly would be reordered and restocked while those items that were slow to sell were discontinued. The practice of stocktaking was an in-depth examination of the business enterprise to determine what changes were required to make it fiscally sound and financially solvent. As our conversation ended, my curiosity was piqued as to how this principle and practice could be applied to human beings. Could human beings 'take stock' while seeking to make their lives more meaningful and more productive? It seems to me that just as management can utilize the process of stocktaking to make a business more profitable that individuals could employ the same techniques in order to make their lives more productive and more fulfilling.

Indeed, as human beings, our lives are essentially 'our business...our enterprise'. Therefore, in order to make our lives productive and meaningful, it is imperative that we monitor, evaluate and scrutinize those values, attributes, attitudes, habits and standards which ensure that our lives yield the dividends that allow us to grow, prosper and be successful. This will enable us to be stewards of our fate and custodians of our future.

The ability and the capacity to evaluate and scrutinize our personal lives can only be achieved through rigorous and consistent self-examination. This practice figures prominently in religious circles where members are urged to search their hearts, purge their minds or thinking or even to purify their consciences. This process is all designed to identify those factors that are inimical to one's growth and to expunge them. It is designed to search for the pollutants and to extricate them from our lives. Furthermore, this process will help us to fortify, consolidate and conserve those factors which promote growth and development. Self-examination is critical for human growth, self-empowerment and personal survival.

Indeed, the Greek Philosopher Socrates has been credited with the famous declarative statement, "the unexamined life is not worth living". In fact, Socrates chose death when confronted with the alternative to live a life in which he was deprived of the opportunity to manage his own life and to be the overseer of his destiny. Socrates was an avid proponent of the idea that through access to knowledge and wisdom a person would be equipped to take control of his or her life. To ensure that this would become a reality Socrates dedicated his life to provide the opportunity for people to have access to this knowledge and wisdom. Obviously, such action ran counter to the will and expectations of the authorities and the establishment of his time. This ostensibly reduced people to be manipulated by the state and to be consigned to a status of subservience. Socrates vigorously opposed this custom, and he continued to educate people to impart knowledge and wisdom to them. Obviously, this brought him in conflict with the state which accused him of corrupting the populace, especially the youth. The punishment meted out to him gave him the option of death or exile. He chose death on the premise that when a person cannot make decisions and judgements about the course and direction of his or her life or is denied the opportunity to make amendments to their lives through self-examination, reflection and introspection then such a life is not worth living because it's a life of perpetual enslavement – hence his declaration that "the unexamined life is not worth living". Socrates believed strongly that as human beings it is our inherent right to be in control of our personal destiny and in order to accomplish this, we must have the means and the capacity and capability to manage our lives. Central and endemic to this role was the ability to examine and evaluate our lives and to make the changes for our development and growth. If we are to reach our destiny we must know when to stay the course and when to change the course. From Socrates we learn that our lives are literally in our hands. We cannot be just passive players, bystanders or spectators relative to the direction of our lives. We are the managers, masters of our future and what we wish to become.

Consistent with this thinking is the recognition that the outcome of your life, that which you desire to become is not inherited, gifted, predetermined or predestined this responsibility must rest upon your shoulders. The quality of life is not a lottery that can be won by chance, circumstance or luck it must be earned through personal effort. It is not fate or some external or supernatural force such as the stars that will shape and determine the outcome of your future. It is a personal responsibility which we must embrace. This is expressed most dramatically by Cassius in an exchange with Brutus in Shakespeare's Julius Caesar that our station and status in life are largely determined by our personal efforts and not by an external force. "Men at some times are masters of their fate, the fault dear Brutus is not in our stars but in ourselves that we are underlings." Once we accept the fact that we are the architects of the life which we want to build and the quality of the life which we hope to experience then it is imperative that we develop a plan to manage our lives. This can only be accomplished through a careful examination of the actions which we take to make our life viable and valuable. As we aspire to become better, more fruitful and productive individuals, we should acknowledge and recognize the importance of and the need for personal reflection and introspection. It is virtually looking into the proverbial mirror, looking deep within ourselves to evaluate all facets of our being with the ultimate goal to do better, to be better and to ensure that our actions are consistent with these objectives. While this self-examination should be rigorous it need not be rigid. It should not be sporadic but intentional. Self-examination is much deeper than the casual new year resolution. It should be multifaceted in nature looking at all areas of our lives such as our health, our relationships, our habits, our attitudes and even our finances. On the one hand, we may discover that we need to make changes, that there may be dreams that have eluded us, attitudes that fail us, habits that threaten to destroy us, and words – our way of communication - that can poison and undermine our relationships and interactions with others. Like the store manager during stock taking we will be required to take decisive actions to remove them from our emotional shelves. On the other hand, during the process of self-examination we may discover the need to reinforce and strengthen those values which help us not only to survive but to thrive.

At all times our ultimate goal is not simply to be engaged in the pursuit of happiness but to strive for its actual achievement which will bring us to a place of renewal and restoration.

CHAPTER 15

TIME IS YOUR MOST PRECIOUS GIFT, BUT IT IS FLEETING, USE IT WISELY.

———◦◦◦———

*"There is a tide in the affairs of men, which when taken
at the flood leads on to fortune. Omitted, all the voyage
of their life is bound in shallows and in miseries, on
such a full sea are we now afloat, and we must take
the current when it serves, or lose our ventures"
William Shakespeare, Julius Caesar Act IV Scene III*

I am sure that if we were given the chance to review our lives and especially the actions which we took and the decisions which we made, that a considerable number of us would conclude that we might have done some things differently particularly in the area of missed opportunities or opportunities in which we failed to take the advantage which they afforded us. To use some of the words by Frank Sinatra's song we may discover that we have more than a few regrets. In essence, we might wish that we were better stewards of our time and use it more wisely, prudently and productively. How often we have heard the warning. Time is of the essence. To a large extent we are who we are based upon the stewardship of our time and the opportunities which we seized.

The ancient Greeks were so conscious of the importance of time that in order to avoid any ambiguity around the different nuances in expressing time, that they used two words which conveyed the sharp and profound distinction between the quantitative and the qualitative nature of time. The two words Kairos and Chronos. Chronos refers to chronological or sequential time such as hours, days or months. Kairos is an ancient Greek word meaning the right, critical or opportune moment. There are times in our lives that are pregnant with opportunities and we must be able to capitalize on those moments if we are to make progress and be successful. We speak of these special moments or time in familiar words such as 'when the time is ripe or in the fullness of time'. That is the translation of Kairos. If we discern and seize these propitious moments, then we are able to capitalize on them and move forward with success. On the contrary, a failure to grasp and grab these opportunities will inevitably result in defeat and failure.

History is replete with idiomatic sayings and aphorisms which are designed to challenge and warn people not only about the importance of both recognizing and seizing those propitious moments that can bring success but of the dire consequence of failing to make use of the opportunities which we encounter in life experiences. Many of us grew up with the memorable words our teachers, parents and others who sought to teach us lessons about the critical importance of time. They utilize the Latin idiom "tempus fugit" time flies or "carpe diem" seize the day or seize the opportunity. We knew intuitively what they were seeking to convey. Many have employed several rich metaphors which graphically convey and depict the priceless consequences of judicious and prudent use of time or the alternative damage of delaying or ignoring the "moment".

I would like to unpack three of the most common metaphorical expressions relating to the prudent and productive use of time. The first being, "make hay while the sun shines". Most of us got the gist of what this aphorism seeks to convey, however, when we probe more deeply into its origins, we get a clear idea of the potency of what it seeks to articulate. At harvest time when farmers were gathering in their wheat they would use the stalk of the wheat as hay for feeding their animals. It was the warmth of the sun that dried up the stalks and turned them into hay. If it rained these stalks would be ruined due to rot and would be useless. Any delay or neglect would jeopardize any prospect of having hay to feed the animals. The message here is that the proper use of time can make all the difference. Failure to act expeditiously at the appropriate time can ruin any chance of success. We can only make hay while the sun is shining.

The second metaphor uses the imagery of the blacksmith "strike while the iron is hot". The work of the blacksmith was to change and shape metals into any object which he wished to produce. In order to accomplish this, he had to apply heat to the metal and as it becomes hot, it is more pliable and subject to be molded into any form. However, when it cools it becomes resistant to change. The message here is clear. We must act decisively and take advantage of an opportunity as soon as it exists, if that opportunity is missed, the chances are lost. This gives credence to the saying that opportunities lost can never be recalled.

The third metaphor conjures up the imagery of the captain setting out to sea at the most favorable time. "There is a tide in the affairs of men. Which when taken at the flood, leads on to fortune; Omitted, all the voyage of their life is bound in shallows and in miseries. On such a full sea are we now afloat; And we must take the current when it serves or lose our ventures." Before the invention of the steam engine, ships were totally dependent upon the conditions of the weather, particularly the tide, for successful sailing. Ships usually needed high tides to enter or leave a port. Failure to set sail when the tide was highest could result in disastrous consequences. It is consistent with the thinking of the dangers of failure to recognize and seize the opportunities of life that Brutus in Shakespeare's Julius Caesar is warning his comrade about the importance of capitalizing on the opportunities to engage in a war or suffering defeat because of inaction. They were on the threshold of being engaged in a civil war, an armed conflict. Brutus is here reminding his partner in the war that delay and procrastination would ensure inevitable defeat while victory would be guaranteed if they took advantage of the opportunities opened to them. This conviction and philosophy underscore the truism of the maxim that "time and tide wait for no man".

Procrastination and delay are the enemies of progress and success. In fact, procrastination is considered to be a self-defeating behavioral pattern that can have a negative impact on all facets of human life. Its consequences and costs can affect all areas of a person's life including their emotional and physical wellbeing. For instance, it can induce stress and insomnia which can further compromise one's immune system and ultimately leads to a downward spiral in ill health. Procrastination can also expand and extend its tentacles to jeopardize our relationships both personal and professional. The best way to defeat this enemy of time is to develop a deeper appreciation for those unique opportunities which time engenders and to take a proactive, aggressive and decisive action to seize and capitalize on the promise which they offer us. We can begin by paying more attention to our health. We are aware that when we neglect our health, we will truly lose the opportunity to enjoy life to its fullest. We should never postpone the attention to our health, the consequence could be fatal. How often have we failed to embrace the moments which we have to repair broken relationships, to seek forgiveness from someone that we have harmed or offended or to offer pardon to someone that has caused us some hurt. The process of healing can only begin with the willingness for reconciliation. Procrastination in this area will only cheat us of our sense of healing. The price of delay will only perpetuate bitterness, brokenness and estrangement.

Another area of our lives that requires attention but too often is ignored until it is too late is making provision for retirement in a timely matter. Too many people fail to make adequate provisions for their retirement, they delay, defer and postpone this inevitable rite of passage. They end up with inadequate resources to meet and supply their needs and this detracts from their sense of happiness, or as Brutus would describe their condition, "their lives are bound in shallows and in miseries. At all times we must take the current when it comes. What should propel and spur us into action is the fact that these special opportunities in our lives are not inexhaustible and above all we must come to terms with the transient and fleeting nature of our humanity. Our time is limited. The span of our years are little more than three score years and ten. Therefore, we are challenged to acknowledge the urgency of the moment with the conviction that life is short and above all that opportunities lost can never be recalled.

Finally, we must not only be able to discern the critical moments which present themselves to us, we should also be cognizant of the fact that we can only take advantage from them if we possess the ability and capacity to do so. The farmer, the blacksmith and the captain of the ship will only be able to benefit from these opportunities if they possess the appropriate skills and training in the area of their vocation. Preparation and planning must be prerequisites that will enable us to use our time wisely, that time which is a precious gift of life even if it is fleeting. While we have time let us do good not only for our own personal benefit but for the benefit of others.